Military Strategy: A Very Short Introduction

Very Short Introductions available now:

Available soon:

For more information visit our website

www.oup.com/vsi/

Antulio J. Echevarria II

MILITARY STRATEGY

A Very Short Introduction

SECOND EDITION

OXFORD
UNIVERSITY PRESS

Oxford University Press is a department of the University of Oxford.
It furthers the University's objective of excellence in research, scholarship,
and education by publishing worldwide. Oxford is a registered trade mark of
Oxford University Press in the UK and in certain other countries.

Published in the United States of America by Oxford University Press
198 Madison Avenue, New York, NY 10016, United States of America.

© Oxford University Press 2013, 2024

Library of Congress Cataloging-in-Publication Data

Names: Echevarria, Antulio J., II, 1959- author.
Title: Military strategy : a very short introduction / Antulio J. Echevarria II.
Description: Second edition. | New York, NY : Oxford University Press, 2024. |
Series: Very short introductions | Includes bibliographical references and index.
Identifiers: LCCN 2023057079 (print) | LCCN 2023057080 (ebook) |
ISBN 9780197760154 (paperback) | ISBN 9780197760178 (epub) |
Subjects: LCSH: Strategy. | Military art and science.
Classification: LCC U162 .E35 2024 (print) | LCC U162 (ebook) |
DDC 355.4—dc23/eng/20240104
LC record available at https://lccn.loc.gov/2023057079
LC ebook record available at https://lccn.loc.gov/2023057080

Integrated Books International, United States of America

Contents

List of illustrations

Prologue

A brief verbal exchange that purportedly took place between an American colonel and a North Vietnamese colonel in 1975 during the negotiations that ended the Vietnam War illustrates the importance of good military strategy. The American colonel, Harry G. Summers Jr., said, "You know you never defeated us on the battlefield." His North Vietnamese counterpart, Colonel Tu, paused a moment, then replied, "That may be so, but it is also irrelevant."

This exchange is often cited—perhaps too often—to highlight shortcomings in U.S. strategic thinking during the Vietnam War. Winning wars is not just a matter of winning battles. One needs a military strategy capable of making one's victories count. The United States spent valuable resources winning many of the key battles in the Vietnam conflict only to lose the war, and the assumptions underpinning U.S. military strategy were partly to blame.

No military strategy can guarantee victory, but an inappropriate one all but ensures failure. Even if a decisive success is beyond one's grasp, a suitable military strategy can increase the odds of a favorable outcome. Military strategy is relevant to any type of conflict, or use of force. Novel technologies, such as nuclear weapons or cyberspace, have brought new possibilities and constraints into being, but they have not diminished the importance of having a good strategy.

Chapter 1
What is military strategy?

Military strategy is the practice of reducing an adversary's physical capacity and willingness to fight, and continuing to do so until one's aim is achieved. It takes place in wartime as well as peacetime and may involve using force, directly or indirectly, as a threat. Reducing an opponent's capacity and willingness to fight is always a relative matter; one can achieve it by building a quantitative or qualitative superiority in military power well before hostilities might commence.

Although historically people have defined military strategy, or strategy, in various ways, the principal task of the strategist has remained virtually the same. Simply put, that task consists in countering the strengths and exploiting the weaknesses of an opponent in ways that make accomplishing one's purpose ever more likely. In practice, strategy comes down to out-positioning one's rivals, not just militarily, but also diplomatically and, if possible, economically and culturally, even before the first clash of arms and often well after hostilities have ceased. This is true whether the struggle is global or local in scope and whether it involves the highest or least of stakes.

Regardless of scope, scale, or aim, military strategy begins with appreciating the strengths and weaknesses of an adversary as they relate to one's own, and to what one wants. It often requires revising one's aims and improvising one's courses of action as the struggle progresses. It ends when one party, or the other, has had enough or literally can do no more.

Classifying military strategy

History's military strategists have described their practice in diverse but informative ways. The ancient Chinese military thinker Sun Tzu discussed strategy in terms of gaining material and moral advantages such that a battle is won before it is fought. Others, such as Antoine-Henri de Jomini, a Swiss military theorist and erstwhile member of Napoleon's staff, referred to it as "making war on the map," that is, maneuvering for positional advantages. The nineteenth-century Prussian military writer Carl von Clausewitz drew a sharp distinction between tactics and strategy: he defined the former is the use of armed forces to win engagements; the latter is the "use of engagements to achieve the purpose of the war." Other German military leaders, such as Count Helmuth von Moltke, the chief of the general staff of the Prussian army in the nineteenth century, portrayed strategy as opportunely adapting to war's changing circumstances until victory is achieved. By comparison, the twentieth-century British military critic Sir Basil Liddell Hart defined strategy as "the art of distributing and applying military means to fulfill the ends of policy." On the other hand, the eminent British scholar Lawrence Freedman suggests strategy may well be the art of generating power.

Some modern historians refer to strategy as a long-term vision and stress its attendant need for planning and decision making. Contemporary strategic theorists such as Colin Gray represent it metaphorically, as a bridge linking political aims and military means, while historian Hew Strachan prefers to underscore the importance of strategic dialogue in reconciling what is desired with what can be done. Still others characterize strategy as the intellectual architecture that gives structure and coherence to one's efforts in wartime or peacetime.

Definitions of strategy are indeed many, and experts sometimes muddle the difference between military strategy and strategy in general. Yet these various definitions are not necessarily unhelpful or contradictory. Each, in fact, refracts strategy through a specific historical and political lens or context, but each also captures recurring themes and activities inseparable from the practice of strategy. Not surprisingly, that practice has evolved with the conduct of war. Jomini's definition of strategy, for instance, deviated little from what the Renaissance political and military writer Niccolò Machiavelli referred to centuries earlier as the art of war. Indeed, the terms *strategy* and *art* or *conduct* of war have been nearly synonymous at times. Nonetheless, from Hannibal's war against Rome to Vladimir Putin's aggression in Ukraine, the practice of military strategy has always come down to finding ways to weaken an adversary's material capacity and willingness to fight with respect to one's aims.

To throw sharper relief on the characteristics of military strategy, we can compare it to what some experts call grand strategy. Military strategy refers to the "business," or concern, of the general, a phrase long associated with the eighth-century Greek word *stratēgia*, which, in turn, captures the spirit of two other Greek terms: *stratēgikē epistēmē* (generals' knowledge) and *stratēgōn sophia* (generals' wisdom). *Stratēgia* was thus a combination of objective knowledge and subjective skill. By comparison, grand strategy can be thought of as the "concern of the head of state" of which the general's business is but one aspect.

Both grand strategists and military strategists endeavor to out-position rival powers irrespective of whether one's goal is offensive or defensive in nature. Grand strategists normally do so by building alliances and coalitions, or by securing treaties and agreements aimed at increasing or preserving one's power relative to one's rivals. Military commanders make use of the material and psychological advantages made available through such partnerships and agreements to develop specific military strategies. Grand strategists weigh the potential costs of an impending armed conflict against its expected benefits, and they attempt to set conditions that will minimize the former and maximize the latter. They also balance concurrent military commitments against long-term interests, and they set priorities accordingly. Military strategists, then, work to achieve success without allowing costs to exceed benefits, or permitting short-term interests to compromise longer range ones.

Ideally, a military strategy should be formulated within the parameters established by a grand strategy so the objectives and priorities of each can be rationalized. However, both levels of strategy function more or less as "open systems," with players and variables changing frequently. As a consequence, military strategy sometimes drives grand strategy or simply operates independently of it. This situation can occur even when military strategy and grand strategy are embodied in the same person, as was the case with Napoleon. Such arrangements can offer benefits with respect to unity of effort, but they can also bring serious disadvantages by overburdening a single decision maker. At other times, military strategy might be hampered by an indecisive grand strategy. Carthage's council of elders, for instance, remained divided between landed interests, which wanted to acquire territories in Africa, and maritime interests, which sought to increase Carthage's influence in the Mediterranean Sea. This division ultimately undercut Carthage's political will and determination in its series of wars against Rome.

In today's defense literature, the term *grand strategy* can refer to alliance or coalition strategy or to national strategy (or national security strategy). Alliance or coalition strategies identify objectives and courses of action for multinational partnerships such as the North Atlantic Treaty Organization (NATO). National strategy sets forth goals to be achieved by the sum of a party's power: its diplomatic, economic, military, and informational resources. For example, the West's grand strategy of "containment" during the

Cold War served both as an alliance strategy for NATO and as a national security strategy for the United States.

Military strategy's equivalent in contemporary defense literature is national military strategy, and it may include any number of supporting strategies for individual regions or theaters. A national military strategy describes how a state will use its military power in pursuit of its policy goals. A regional or theater strategy specifies how military resources are to be used to achieve objectives within a given geographic area. The national military strategies supporting containment, for instance, included deterrence in central Europe and on the Korean Peninsula, as well as several types of coercive strategies carried out in the Middle East and Latin America. Military strategy is thus frequently nested or tiered, particularly when the endeavor is a global one and multiple parties are involved.

Crafting military strategy

Modern defense analysts often divide military strategy (and grand strategy) into three essential components: *ends* (objectives) + *ways* (courses of action) + *means* (resources). This model was advanced by Arthur F. Lykke Jr., an engineer by training, who taught a generation of military professionals in the United States. Ends or objectives may include intimidating, deterring, persuading, coercing, punishing, subduing, or conquering an adversary. Ways are essentially types of military strategy, or combinations of them. Means equate to military power. An example of how these components fit together is NATO's military strategy in central Europe: its objective (*end*) was to deter an attack by the Warsaw Pact, and it was accomplished by maintaining formidable defensive postures (*way*) involving nuclear weapons and a combination of conventional and special forces (*means*).

Some analysts add the element of risk to Lykke's equation. A good strategy is said to be one in which all three components

5

(ends, ways, and means) are in balance, that is, the means are sufficient to accomplish the ends through the designated ways. The basic rationale for balance is it reduces risk. However, military commanders tend to view risk differently from heads of state, and it is important to understand why. Commanders define risk as the likelihood a mission might fail: high risk means high probability of failure. They usually try to reduce risk by increasing resources in some way. In contrast, heads of state view risk as a function of the political capital they might have to invest, or have already invested. Put simply, political capital is the trust and confidence the public has in its leadership. As the commitment of resources (lives and treasure) increases, so too does the risk to political capital. Accordingly, political leaders prefer to keep the resources they commit to a military action, especially human lives, as low as possible.

Today, representing strategy as ends + ways + means + risk is common in defense circles. It offers policymakers and military personnel a basic framework for discussing the particulars of a strategy, especially whether the resources are adequate for the desired ends. However, no scientific method exists for determining how much military power is enough, or when balance is achieved. The answer depends largely on the professional judgment of military commanders, and on what domestic conditions will allow in terms of the expenditure of fiscal resources and political capital. In truth, balance, like beauty, is in the eye of the beholder.

In fact, the Lykke equation or structure provides little more than a starting point for planning. One could use it to build a bridge or any complex edifice, for instance. What distinguishes a strategy from a plan is the nature of the environment and the presence of an adversary or a rival. If the environment is competitive and an adversary is present, one needs a strategy; otherwise, a plan will suffice.

Practicing military strategy

Experts have long debated whether military strategy is an art or a science, and they will probably continue to do so for ages to come. Today's military strategists would do better to think of it as a practice; it combines the objective knowledge of science (insofar as it can be objective) with the subjective knowledge (or skill) associated with an art. The practice of military strategy, or any type or level of strategy for that matter, can be thought of as applying technical knowledge, or an understanding of what is possible, and social intelligence, or a sense of what is likely in regard to human behavior, to achieve one's aim. Put differently, the ends-ways-means-risk equation assumes one has an appreciation for military power, what it can and cannot do, and an understanding of some of the fundamental types of military strategy and how they can be linked to form operations and campaigns to achieve what one wants.

Military power can be defined as the ability to perform specific combat missions in a given situation. For example, a force consisting of nuclear submarines and cruise missiles would offer little useful military power in a situation calling for counterinsurgency techniques. Likewise, a well-equipped but poorly trained militia might offer little in the way of genuine military power against a similarly equipped, but better trained, regular force.

Like all forms of power, military power is inherently multidimensional. It is typically categorized as land power, sea power, air power (or aerospace power), and informational and (more recently) cyber power. Land power is the ability of one's ground forces to exert control over centers of authority and influence, which are usually based on land. Sea power can be thought of as the ability to control maritime lines of communication and commerce, and to project military forces ashore. Aerospace power typically refers to two domains, air and space (to orbital distances) and the ability to operate within and project force from them. Informational power has come to include what was once referred to as propaganda and psychological warfare but has now evolved into the much larger category of strategic communications. Information can magnify, or in some cases dampen, the repercussive effects of physical force, and it can also help cultivate useful impressions among targeted audiences. Cyber power is the ability to operate with relative security within cyberspace, and it is usually associated with the ability to facilitate or impede the flow of information or code.

Military power can be augmented by what analysts call principles of war or principles of operations. These principles are sometimes characterized as timeless and universal, but they are not necessarily either. Although they can offer advantages to one party or the other, the extent to which they do so is driven largely by the situation. The following nine principles appear most frequently in professional military literature: (1) *objective*, defining the goal and ensuring that every military action contributes toward achieving it; (2) *maneuver*, gaining positional advantage; (3) *surprise*, attacking one's foe in an unexpected manner; (4) *mass*, concentrating military power to achieve superiority; and its converse (5) *economy of force*, ensuring that secondary efforts receive only as much force as necessary; (6) *offensive*, gaining the initiative or the temporal upper-hand; (7) *security*, ensuring that one's forces are well protected; (8) *simplicity*, avoiding complicated schemes and communications; and (9) *unity of command*, placing the direction of the war under a single political-military authority to avoid conflicting interests.

The elements of military power are interdependent, and combining them usually enhances the potency of each. Airpower, for instance, can make some of the tasks armies and navies must accomplish that much easier; armies and navies, in turn, can provide the staying power that air forces lack. Also, military power is rarely used in isolation. It is normally employed in conjunction with some degree of diplomatic, informational, and economic or financial power. Military leaders might not exercise direct control over all these elements in democratic societies, but that is not necessarily the case in other societies. In any event, strategists must understand how these elements work individually and in combination with others.

There are many types of military strategy. Among the most common historically are annihilation, dislocation, attrition, exhaustion, coercion, deterrence, terror and terrorism, and decapitation and targeted killing. Each is worth exploring further.

Annihilation and dislocation represent the "ideal outcome" in military strategy: a swift victory with as few friendly casualties and economic costs as possible. These strategies often work hand-in-glove, and therefore they can be difficult to distinguish from one another in practice. However, the key difference is annihilation seeks to reduce an adversary's physical capacity to fight, usually in a single battle or "lightning" campaign; on the other hand, dislocation endeavors to reduce an opponent's willingness to fight by causing confusion or disorientation through an unexpected maneuver or the use of surprise. Both can employ operational maneuvers, such as double or single envelopments or increased tempo.

Attrition and exhaustion are the polar opposites of annihilation and dislocation. Attrition means reducing an adversary's physical capacity to fight; exhaustion amounts to wearing down the opponent's willingness to do so. Again, a close relationship exists between the two, which can make them difficult to distinguish in practice. Nevertheless, the basic difference is that attrition assumes an opponent's willingness to resist is strong and will not break until its physical capacity to do so is eliminated. Conversely, exhaustion assumes a party's willingness to resist is weak and can be broken well before its physical capacity to do so is destroyed.

Unlike annihilation and dislocation, these strategies accept that the process of defeating an opponent may take considerable time. Hence, they are less than ideal for most societies because they put an enormous and prolonged strain on one's own material capacity and morale. Nonetheless, they are important because many strategies devolve into one or the other of these two, and thus it is not always possible to avoid them. As some experts maintain, attrition and exhaustion represent the most fundamental, if also the most brutal, of military strategies, and all other types may well be but variations of these two.

Compellence and deterrence, two basic components of coercion strategies, occur not just in wartime but also in peacetime. In fact, if a war breaks out it can mean one or both strategies has failed in its initial aims. Compellence simply means forcing adversaries to do something, while deterrence is dissuading opponents from doing something. Together, these strategies constitute the fundamental dynamic driving most peacetime and wartime situations, at the highest echelons of diplomacy as well as the lowest levels of tactics. Interestingly, very little of the vast literature concerning these two strategies treats them as a single, but linked, dynamic. From the standpoint of military strategy, it is rarely sufficient to compel one's foes to do something; usually one must also deter them from doing something else. Counterterrorism and counterinsurgency campaigns, for instance, are contemporary examples of this dynamic at work: the aim is to neutralize hostile terrorist groups or insurgents, but to do so in ways that do not add to their recruitment efforts.

Strategies of terror and terrorism endeavor to succeed by leveraging fear. Strategies of terror include the aerial bombing of a hostile party's vital centers so as to cause its population to demand peace. Terrorism has many varieties, but in general it endeavors to compel a change in a party's behavior by instilling fear either through selective targeting or through mass targeting of noncombatants. Both terror and terrorism have decidedly coercive aspects, but each also has a deterrent capacity because each can bring about a desire not to act. Whether terrorism constitutes a strategy or a tactic is still a matter of debate for some scholars. However, recent research suggests using terror tactics over a prolonged period of time to shape the public's perceptions and to change its behavior equates to a strategy.

The use of decapitation and targeted killing has increased markedly since the beginning of the twenty-first century, particularly with the widespread production of remotely piloted vehicles or drones. Decapitation and targeted killing derive from dislocation and attrition, respectively. Decapitation is the attempt to paralyze or collapse a group by removing its leadership. Targeted killing is the systematic elimination of an organization's members, whether these individuals occupy key positions or belong to the rank and file. Both strategies are controversial due to because of questions regarding how effective and ethical they truly are.

Cyberspace not only augments traditional military strategies, it also provides opportunities to win without fighting. Cyber power has contributed to the conduct of major wars and conflicts against violent nonstate actors. However, it remains controversial because its contributions have produced only temporary effects and have not brought about quick, decisive victories. Yet its potential for successful social manipulation is only in its early stages.

Technology is vital to the practice of military strategy because it speaks to one's means. The means obviously influence the ways, or what one can do. In any assessment it is essential to ask how particular technologies might influence one's ability to out-position one's rivals. Biotechnology and nanotechnology are two emerging fields that will surely alter the practice of strategy; however, cyberspace has already done so. Today's strategists need to worry less about whether there is such a thing as "cyber war," which experts continue to debate, and more about how to achieve and maintain cyber power and how to leverage it to augment military strategy.

Practicing military strategy successfully frequently requires dividing the conflict into phases or campaigns, the sum of which should culminate in achieving the war's purpose. In practicing military strategy, we might design a battle of encirclement and annihilation as part of a campaign of dislocation, which, in turn, might contribute to an overall strategy of attrition or exhaustion designed to coerce our opponent into agreeing to our terms. The art or business of the general, in other words, has as much to do with understanding how each of these strategies works individually as well as how they might be combined for best effect.

Chapter 2
Annihilation and dislocation

As Sun Tzu once said, "Victory is the main object in war. If this is
long delayed, weapons are blunted and morale depressed." For this
reason, most parties want to win quickly. The military strategies of
annihilation and dislocation are classic ways of succeeding swiftly.
Annihilation strategies aim to do so by severely reducing or
eliminating an opponent's material strength through one or two
major battles. Such battles usually entail encircling an adversary's
military force or enveloping its flanks. Some examples, discussed
in more detail below, include Hannibal's victory over the Romans
on the plains of Cannae in 216 BCE, Napoleon's defeat of the
Austrians and Russians in 1805 and the Prussians in 1806, and
the American destruction of Spanish flotillas at Manila Bay and
Santiago Bay in 1898. Notable twentieth-century generals, such as
Erwin Rommel and Norman Schwartzkopf, are known to have
compared some of their own victories to Cannae. However,
Cannae also represents the classic pitfall of winning battles only to
lose wars since Rome eventually overcame its staggering losses
and finally defeated Carthage 14 years later at the battle
of Zama.

Whereas annihilation strategies seek to win by destroying an
opponent's physical capacity to resist, dislocation strategies
endeavor to achieve victory through an unexpected maneuver that
achieves surprise and knocks an adversary off balance

psychologically. A classic case of dislocation, described in more detail below, is Hitler's so-called blitzkrieg campaign against France in 1940. The Germans did not have better technology than the French or British; nor were they necessarily better led. However, they managed to achieve surprise by attacking through the Ardennes Forest, which many considered impassable for motorized formations, and then to strike that part of the Allied lines least prepared for it.

Neither annihilation nor dislocation necessitates massive bloodletting or complete destruction. Sometimes destruction is unnecessary because the shock effect created by encircling or unhinging an adversary's formations leads to surrender in great numbers. Each of these strategies usually requires military forces trained well enough, and led effectively enough, to execute complex maneuvers. As Sun Tzu said centuries ago, "Both advantage and danger are inherent in maneuver." A course of action that promises great advantage usually entails great risk as well.

Annihilation

The battle of Cannae is the classic example of annihilation through a double envelopment. Most military professionals are familiar with it, and many academies and staff colleges include it in their courses on tactics and strategy. Nonetheless, the battle's popularity is, in many respects, unfortunate because Cannae did not decide the war in favor of Carthage. Hannibal's army (50,000) confronted a larger Roman force (80,000) under Caius Terentius Varro that was formed up on a frontage too narrow for its numbers. Hannibal took advantage of this error by inviting attack in the center, where he positioned his light infantry (mostly Gauls), while his veteran-heavy infantry (mostly Africans) formed up in columns along the flanks.

Varro accommodated Hannibal by attacking in the center and succeeded in putting his head into the noose the Carthaginian commander had prepared. Hannibal's light infantry fell back as the Roman formations advanced. The Carthaginian heavy infantry then closed on the Romans from the wings, while its cavalry, which had driven off its Roman counterpart, attacked the rear, completing the encirclement.

The legions were too disorganized and confined within too small a space to form coherent battle lines, and the fighting thus quickly became one-sided to the benefit of the Carthaginians. At the end of the day, Roman losses numbered some 50,000 dead, with another 20,000 captured. Approximately 10,000 managed to break out of the encirclement and flee the area with Varro. Hannibal lost nearly 6,000 dead, or about 12 percent of his army, and an unknown number of wounded. It was a costly victory, but one the Carthaginian general evidently expected would bring Rome to the negotiating table. By this time, Hannibal had been fighting Rome for nearly two years, and he had killed or wounded some 100,000 legionnaires, more than 10 percent of Rome's male population of military age.

Contrary to Hannibal's expectations, the victory at Cannae, devastating as it was, did not lead Rome to surrender. Historical evidence, scant though it may be, suggests Hannibal did not aim to destroy Rome but merely to reduce its power and influence, while at the same time restoring the prestige and influence that Carthage had lost in the first Punic War (264–241 BCE). Historians believe two concessions would have satisfied Hannibal: an indemnity from Rome and the return of some of Carthage's Mediterranean islands, namely Corsica and Sicily. Yet the Roman senate voted not to negotiate, perhaps fearing Hannibal's terms would prove as harsh as their own usually were, or believing Roman losses, which had been severe indeed, had to be avenged.

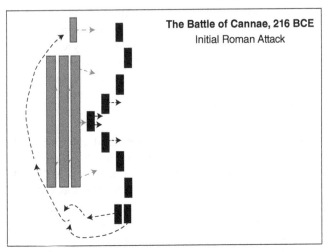

The Battle of Cannae, 216 BCE
Initial Roman Attack

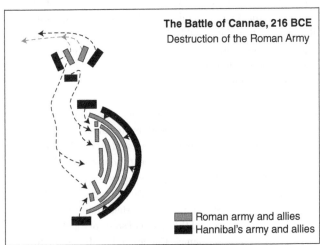

The Battle of Cannae, 216 BCE
Destruction of the Roman Army

Roman army and allies
Hannibal's army and allies

1. During the battle of Cannae, Hannibal deploys his troops in a manner that invites the impetuous Roman general Varro to launch a frontal attack; Hannibal's center then retreats, drawing the legions in deeper while the Carthaginian heavy infantry and cavalry attack the wings and close the trap. Cannae represents the classic strategy of annihilation through a battle of encirclement.

Either way, Hannibal's assumptions regarding what it would take to subdue Rome proved wrong. To be sure, the battle did not win the war, but to say there was little strategic effect is misleading. The victory at Cannae clearly put Hannibal in a better strategic position than he had been beforehand. Several Greek colonies and Italian city-states defected immediately to the Carthaginian cause, giving Hannibal bases from which to operate and supply his troops. Although he was also obliged to defend those bases, they created a situation of rough strategic parity that enabled Hannibal to add troops to his army at about the same rate the Romans could raise new legions.

Hannibal's victory at Cannae clearly did not bring about the result he desired. However, it did place Carthage in a better position strategically for the next phase of the war, which involved a protracted struggle for influence with each side endeavoring to attract allies. Certainly, Hannibal's initial military strategy rested on an incorrect assumption about his opponent, and he lacked an appealing alternative in the event it proved false. Nonetheless, his error—the "Hannibalic fallacy," as it is called—lay less in failing to use his victory to full effect, as critics such as the Roman historian Livy later claimed, but rather in expecting his enemy to act in a certain way, the way belligerents had traditionally behaved after a defeat of such magnitude. In any case, Carthage's failure to win the war was due more to the ambivalence of its grand strategy, which remained fatally divided between landed interests, favoring expansion into Africa, and maritime interests, desiring greater influence along the Mediterranean basin.

A case when a strategy of envelopment and annihilation did win the war is Napoleon's Ulm campaign. It was carried out in the autumn of 1805 against Austrian general Karl Mack von Leiberich. Facing an armed conflict against an Austrian and Russian coalition, Napoleon decided to take the offensive and to attack the former while the latter were still several weeks away. He sent 40,000 troops across the Rhine River near Strasbourg to fix the attention of the Austrians, while the remainder of his army (160,000) marched eastward and southward, crossing the Danube between Ingolstadt and Münster, to come at the Austrians from behind (*la manoeuvre sur les derrières*).

This maneuver severed General Mack's lines of communication with Vienna and caused a great deal of confusion for the Austrian high command. Mack attempted to break out of the encirclement several times, but he failed in each attempt. He finally surrendered on October 20, 1805, along with 27,000 of his troops; another 30,000 more followed suit shortly thereafter. The envelopment of the Austrian army led to its swift annihilation and bought Napoleon enough time to regroup and prepare for the Russian army (now 85,000 strong), which he soundly defeated at the battle of Austerlitz on December 2, 1805. The victories at Ulm and Austerlitz shattered the Austrian and Russian armies, but they did not result in a durable peace for the French. Again, this was more a failure of grand strategy than military strategy. Napoleon's genius lay more with the latter than the former.

The French victory in the Ulm campaign was due not only to Napoleon's superior generalship, but also to the misjudgments of the "unfortunate General Mack," as he was to refer to himself in the aftermath. Mack's misfortune resulted in part from directing his army based on rumors rather than confirmed intelligence; he drew unwarranted conclusions from hasty and incomplete reports, even allowing himself to be deluded at one point that the French were in full retreat. Napoleon's true intentions remained a mystery to him until it was too late. Mack also lacked a clear sense of the whereabouts of his Russian allies. In addition, Napoleon had a more effective military instrument with which to work. The French army was simply better trained and better led than its Austrian counterpart. It was eminently capable of executing the type of complex maneuver Napoleon had conceived; on the contrary, it is unlikely Mack's army could have done the same had the situation been reversed.

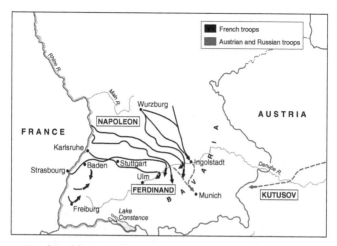

2. Napoleon feigns a major frontal attack across the Rhine River between Freiburg and Baden to fix General Mack's attention, but then swings the bulk of his army against the Austrians' weakly defended right flank and rear areas. The Ulm campaign illustrates a battle of annihilation on a grand scale.

Superior generalship and training are not the only factors that enable one to execute a strategy of annihilation. A severe imbalance in military technology also can increase the odds disproportionately in favor of one side or the other. Such an imbalance was evident in the naval battles between the American and Spanish fleets at Manila Bay, the Philippines, on May 1, 1898, and at Santiago Bay, Cuba, on July 3, 1898. The Spanish flotilla at Manila Bay numbered some 40 vessels, but none qualified as a modern warship. The U.S. Asiatic Squadron (seven warships) had little difficulty annihilating the Spanish, despite being outnumbered and confronted by coastal batteries and underwater mines. The faster American ships were able to make several devastating runs at the Spanish fleet, while evading most of its return fire. Likewise, on July 3 a modern U.S. fleet easily destroyed a Spanish flotilla (four cruisers and two destroyers) as it attempted to escape from Santiago Bay. Intangibles such as bravery and skill are always difficult to weigh and may have been about equal on each side, but the technological superiority of the American vessels was clearly evident and proved decisive.

However, even in this case, the swift annihilation of the bulk of its naval power did not compel the opposing party to sue for peace. Instead, Madrid agreed to terms only after land forces seized Manila and Santiago.

Dislocation

The paradigmatic example of dislocation is perhaps what famously (and incorrectly) became known as "blitzkrieg," or lightning war, during the Second World War. While no official blitzkrieg doctrine actually existed, the German army at the time did have an established theoretical and practical preference for a war of movement (*Bewegungskrieg*) rather than a war of position (*Stellungskrieg*). In the 1920s the German army consciously decided the static, positional warfare of the First World War was an aberration, a situation to be avoided in the future. It decided, instead, to return to the principles that had brought victory in the campaigns against France in 1870–71. Chief among these principles was the idea of relentless forward movement—an unremitting battle, or *Schlacht ohne Morgen* (literally, battle without morning). Once a breakthrough was achieved, the object of a war of movement was to keep an enemy force off balance by constantly moving and attacking so as to retain the initiative and prevent one's opponent from reestablishing a firm defensive line.

However, a war of movement required reliable means of communication between air and ground formations, forward and rear elements, operational and logistical commands, and higher and lower headquarters. Commanders had to be able to take the initiative and to act without orders (but within the framework of the overall scheme of maneuver) whenever communications broke down, as they invariably would. Logistics, in turn, had to be geared to supporting a high tempo of operations, even if that meant forgoing broad advances in favor of narrow penetrations. The concept of battles of encirclement and annihilation blended easily with the fundamental principles of a war of movement. As some analysts and war correspondents at the time observed, the technique of blitzkrieg was based more on the principle of surprise than overwhelming force.

Indeed, the Wehrmacht's early triumphs came from using force in ways opponents did not expect, and for which they were therefore ill-prepared. The fall of France in the spring of 1940 is perhaps the quintessential illustration of this principle. The main thrust of the German attack occurred through the Ardennes Forest, which was considered impassable for large mechanized formations and thus only lightly guarded. As a result, the German advance reached the English Channel ten days after the attack began and severed the lines of communication and supply for several hundred thousand French, British, and Belgian troops. Hours after the German spearheads had reached the coast, Premier Paul Reynaud told the French senate, "Our classic conception of war has come up against a new conception." It was a concept that involved "massive use of heavy armored divisions and cooperation between them and airplanes, but also the creation of disorder in the enemy's rear by parachute raids and by false news and orders by telephone to the civil authorities." Reynaud then added, "Of all the tasks which confront us the most important is clear thinking. We must think of the new type of warfare we are facing and take immediate decisions." By stressing the need for "clear thinking" to deal with a "new" type of warfare, Reynaud's speech betrayed how pronounced and widespread the sense of dislocation had become within the French high command.

One explanation of the German success credits it to the relative swiftness of the Wehrmacht's command structure and operational responsiveness, which seemed better able to adapt to the fluid situations created by maneuver warfare than its French counterpart. This advantage has been referred to as "getting inside an opponent's decision cycle," a phrase that borrows freely from the theories of American fighter pilot and military theorist John R. Boyd. Boyd was trained as a fighter pilot and served in the Korean War, but he apparently never engaged enemy aircraft in combat. Although his later theories drew from various disciplines and aimed at a comprehensive understanding of winning and losing in war, he is most frequently associated with the "OODA" loop, which stands for Observe, Orient, Decide, Act; it basically describes the decision cycle of a fighter pilot in combat: observe the situation, orient on the enemy, decide which course of action to take, and execute it.

In Boyd's view, this decision cycle could be applied to all levels and all types of war (or competitive endeavors, such as business), and the side with a command structure capable of completing this cycle faster than its rival would have a distinct advantage. Ultimately the party with the more cumbersome command structure would find itself issuing orders for situations that no longer existed. Its actions would, in other words, become progressively irrelevant. Some historians believe this irrelevance is what happened to the French command in 1940; by the time it reacted to German movements, it was too late.

Boyd's OODA loop was enthusiastically embraced by maneuver theorists during the 1970s and 1980s, and it partially underpinned the popular maneuver doctrine of the Cold War era called AirLand Battle. This doctrine served as the bedrock for NATO defense policy, and it provided the framework for the coalition victory in Desert Storm (1990–91). These principles harkened back to the tried-and-true precepts of maneuver, but they also allowed for the destructive power of modern weaponry and the ability to synchronize fire and movement throughout the depth of the battle area.

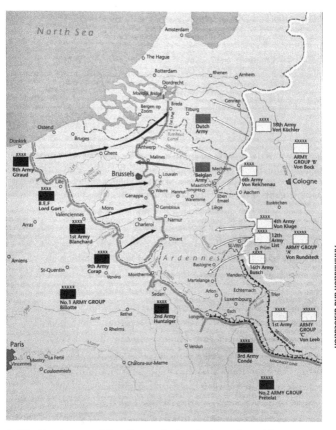

3. The German attack into France during the Second World War disoriented the Allied armies and cut most of their lines of communication and supply by striking from an unexpected direction—through the "impassable" Ardennes Forest. The Ardennes campaign is a definitive example of a strategy of dislocation.

The Simplified OODA Loop

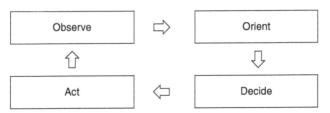

4. Boyd's OODA loop is meant to capture the basic thought processes behind human action: One observes something happening, orients toward it, decides what to do about it, and then acts. Being able to complete this cycle faster than one's opponent gives one an advantage.

The Achilles' heel of Hitler's so-called blitzkrieg wars became abundantly clear during his invasion of the Soviet Union in the summer of 1941. Although massive battles of encirclement occurred, and they netted more than 1 million Soviet prisoners and destroyed thousands of Red Army armored vehicles, the enormous distances covered by the German armies caused the troops and machines to wear down. Moreover, even when encircled some Soviet units fought doggedly rather than surrendering, which delayed the advance of follow-on German formations and replicated the conditions of a war of attrition. Large gaps grew between the panzer spearheads and their supporting foot-borne infantry, whose task it was to reduce the encircled pockets. In truth, the Wehrmacht never possessed the level of mechanization or motorization necessary for such an undertaking. Germany's logistical system, geared more for short, sharp offensives, could not keep pace with the incessant demand for troops and material caused by warfare on the vast Russian steppes.

Strategies of annihilation and dislocation apply most readily to conventional wars. In unconventional conflicts the foe is often too dispersed for an annihilating battle or a dislocating maneuver to take place. Indeed, one of the main objectives of irregular fighters is to avoid being drawn into decisive battles; as Henry Kissinger once wrote, a "conventional army loses if it does not win. The guerrilla wins if he does not lose." Nonetheless, annihilation is not unknown in irregular wars. The Romans put down many revolts swiftly and ruthlessly, though such measures were not always successful. The same uneven pattern is noticeable in the U.S. army's campaigns against Native Americans in the second half of the nineteenth century. The key to success appeared to be to act quickly to isolate an uprising before it could gather momentum and spread, which usually required co-opting or apprehending rebel leaders and their followers while simultaneously restricting or destroying their logistical wherewithal. Mere acts of reprisal alone, as the Romans (and virtually every army since) discovered, often proved counterproductive. Nevertheless, extending olive branches without a supporting display of force was sometimes interpreted as weakness, and it usually encouraged opponents to hold out for a better deal, or to escalate their attacks.

Dislocation and the "indirect approach"

In 1941 the British military critic and theorist Sir B. H. Liddell Hart published a book titled *The Strategy of the Indirect Approach*, in which he endeavored to coin a distinct type of military strategy. The basic idea of the indirect approach is to avoid engaging opponents head-on, in ways they would expect; instead, the goal is to try to dislocate or surprise them by striking in unexpected (hence, indirect) ways. As he explained: "Throughout the ages, effective results in war have rarely been attained unless the approach has had such indirectness as to ensure the opponent's unreadiness to meet it. The indirectness has usually been physical, and always psychological. In strategy, the longest way round is often the shortest way home."

Accordingly, the indirect approach, which the author sometimes reduced to the expression "lure and trap," could be used offensively or defensively. On the defensive, one could use an elastic defense, or calculated withdrawal, to lure opponents into areas where the trap, or counterattack, could be sprung. On the offensive, one could advance to seize areas "upsetting" to one's opponents and thereby inducing them to maneuver themselves into the trap. Liddell Hart's theory of the indirect approach drew from two maxims: direct attacks against strong enemies are never justified; and opponents must be knocked off balance, not by the attack itself, but before it commences. These maxims could be found in most of the military literature published since the late nineteenth century that appreciated the destructive power of modern weaponry and sought ways to avoid or neutralize it. They were also underscored by Liddell Hart's personal experiences on the Western Front during the First World War, particularly during the battle of the Somme in 1916. The truth is that direct attacks are sometimes necessary and are, therefore, justifiable, if undesirable. Moreover, whether a foe actually will be knocked off balance, and for how long, is difficult to predict. Dislocation is usually temporary or felt only at the higher levels of command.

To illustrate his theory, Liddell Hart claimed to have drawn examples from the whole of history, from wars of antiquity to the modern era. He took pains to explain not only when and why the indirect approach succeeded, but also why direct measures fell short. In each case he tried to show how the degree of indirectness corresponded to the degree of victory: the greater the psychological surprise and dislocation, the greater the victory. Such was his argument regarding Hannibal's indirect route over the Alps, and the subsequent battles of annihilation waged by the Carthaginians at Ticinus, Trebia, and Cannae. He said the same about the Roman general Scipio's campaigns in Spain and North Africa leading to the battle of Zama in 202 BCE. Liddell Hart described Napoleon's victories at Ulm and Austerlitz in 1805 as subtle variations of "lure and trap" maneuvers. He also claimed

Ulysses S. Grant's capture of Vicksburg in 1863 and William T. Sherman's campaigns in Georgia in 1864 were instances of the indirect approach applied to "the enemy's economic and moral rear," and that it was this approach that ultimately proved decisive in the American Civil War. In short, his argument became circular: every important success in the history of war was due to some application of the indirect approach— thus, the indirect approach is the surest way to achieve important successes in war.

Despite Liddell Hart's efforts to prove otherwise, history is replete with cases in which avoiding the direct approach ended in disaster or disappointment. Two such examples, both strongly advocated by Winston Churchill, were the aborted Dardanelles campaign during the First World War and the invasion of the Italian Peninsula by Allied forces in the Second World War. The Dardanelles strait connected the Aegean Sea and the Sea of Marmara; a successful landing and campaign there, it was supposed, would threaten Constantinople. Capturing the city might, in turn, knock Turkey out of the war, while also opening a sea lane to southern Russia. In Liddell Hart's view, "While the Dardanelles move was a direct approach to Turkey, it was an indirect approach to the main Turkish armies then engaged in the Caucasus, and, on the higher level, an indirect approach to the Central Powers as a whole." However, the campaign was a disaster, bogging down because of excessive optimism in the high command, poor planning, inadequate reconnaissance, and insufficient logistics; it involved some 500,000 British, French, Australian, New Zealand, and Indian troops, of whom more than half became casualties. Liddell Hart had basically explained away the failure as one of execution rather than of conception.

The Italian campaign (1943–45) was intended as an attack against the "soft underbelly" of Hitler's Fortress Europe. Liddell Hart described it as a success overall because of the diversion of military strength it forced upon the Third Reich. However, subsequent research has thrown doubt on that conclusion due to the rugged nature of the terrain on the peninsula, which favored the defender and slowed the advance of the Allies, increasing their costs in troops and material. The Allies suffered some 320,000 casualties, compared with 430,000 losses incurred by the Axis. The underbelly of the Italian Peninsula proved anything but soft. More to the point, the burden of the war was still being carried by the Soviets on the Eastern Front, who were applying the direct approach with relentless and brutal effectiveness. By late 1943, the Germans were losing approximately one army division per day (13,000 troops) on the Eastern Front. Their losses for the entire Italian campaign were roughly equivalent to one month's fighting on the Eastern Front. Put differently, Hitler could have fought holding actions like the one in Italy for a prolonged period of time.

Over time, Liddell Hart augmented his theory with additional historical illustrations, but its core ideas remained unchanged. To add illustrative weight, he borrowed several aphorisms from the Chinese military philosopher Sun Tzu and incorporated them into the later editions of *Strategy*. Aphorisms such as "All warfare is based on deception" are often seen as the counterpoise to the alleged Western preference for confronting an opponent's main strength directly; such references seemed to lend credence to the indirect approach. However, even a brief survey of Western wars shows an abundant use of deceptions and ruses. Liddell Hart essentially pruned and grafted history to fit his theory, which can be reduced to avoiding the most obvious path to one's aim. Any competent military strategist would prefer to take an opponent by surprise whenever possible. For these reasons, the indirect approach does not actually amount to a distinct military strategy. It can, however, augment other strategies, especially annihilation or dislocation, by increasing their odds of success through the use of unexpected measures.

In sum, annihilation and dislocation can be considered high-risk, high-reward strategies. They hold out the promise of a short war, but they usually require a qualitative or quantitative advantage in military power. They can prove effective against a numerically superior foe, but the maneuvers they are likely to require would prove more complex, and thus entail greater risk. Friction or chance could derail such maneuvers. During the German advance into France in 1940, French reconnaissance flights and Belgian cavalry troops reported considerable enemy motorized and armored formations on the move in the Ardennes Forest. Had Allied air power responded to those reports, it might have wreaked havoc on the lengthy panzer columns inching their way along the forest's narrow roads and the battle for France would have had a very different outcome.

Perhaps the greatest risk, however, lies in assuming a major military victory will prove decisive, and thus end the war in one's favor. That assumption might prove correct if political and cultural conditions are conducive. The shock and humiliation of a swift defeat on the battlefield can induce a government to sue for peace or it can inspire fear and greater resolve. Such resolve might manifest itself as a strategy of attrition or exhaustion, which, in turn, would exploit the vulnerability of a party that must fight a short war.

Chapter 3
Attrition and exhaustion

In early January 1943, just 13 months after the United States was drawn into the Second World War, President Franklin D. Roosevelt told the U.S. Congress: "We set as a primary task in the war of the Pacific a day-by-day and week-by-week and month-by-month destruction of more Japanese war materials than Japanese industry could replace." The military strategy Roosevelt had described to Congress, and that ultimately brought victory to the Allies, was one of attrition. The Allies could afford to pursue such a strategy due to their overwhelming economic and industrial might compared with that of the Axis powers. Simply put, a strategy of attrition aims to win by grinding down an opponent's material strength.

A complement to a strategy of attrition is a strategy of exhaustion, which is wearing down a foe's willingness to fight. Often the two go hand in hand; destroying a party's material strength also can lead to a decline in its willingness to fight. However, sometimes an adversary can be brought to the point of exhaustion by continuing to resist and thereby making the war seem endless or pointless. Vietnamese leader Ho Chi Minh used a strategy of exhaustion to make the French occupation of Indochina too painful for them. On the eve of the first Indochina War (1946–54), Ho boldly warned a French general, though ten Vietnamese will die for every Frenchman killed, the French will tire of the struggle first. With a new French republic struggling to establish itself and to rebuild its economy after the Second World War, the timing was right for Ho's strategy of exhaustion, and his warning proved prophetic. In brief, a strategy of exhaustion endeavors either to make an adversary grow weary of the struggle or to make victory seem impossible. Both strategies can mean lengthy wars, which, in turn, can impose heavy burdens on one's population and economy. Hence, they are not always culturally acceptable or economically practical. However, when they are, they can provide effective counters to strategies of annihilation and dislocation, both of which seek to win quickly. Attrition and exhaustion are often said to form the basis of all other military strategies, and there is some truth to this claim. In fact, every military strategy involves wearing down an adversary's material or psychological strength, or at least threatening to do so. Also, attrition or exhaustion are what typically results when other strategies fail.

The strategy of the Allies in the Second World War is a modern model of attrition. That strategy involved a combination of land, air, and sea campaigns to destroy the military might of the Axis powers faster than it could be replaced, concurrent with the Allies' advance on their capitals. Rome's Fabius Maximus, appropriately nicknamed "Cunctator" (Delayer), used a strategy of exhaustion—known at the time as "hitting the enemy army in the stomach"—to weaken Hannibal's forces logistically. George Washington, referred to by prominent historians as the "American Fabius," also used a form of exhaustion in the American War of Independence to wear down British resolve.

Attrition

Attrition is perhaps the most straightforward of military strategies. In its simplest form it means destroying an opponent's forces faster than they can be replaced, while at the same time ensuring one's own rate of loss remains bearable. Military experts have long agreed a party's willingness to fight and its physical ability to do so are closely linked. The former is considered the most important. Nevertheless, it can be difficult to discern when a party's willingness to fight has actually been broken; it might have experienced a drop in morale that will be only short-lived. Thus, some military strategists prefer courses of action aimed at eliminating a foe's physical capacity to fight, in other words, a strategy of attrition. If a party can be deprived of its weaponry, the conflict can become easier to manage, even if that party refuses to concede. Attrition does not require a favorable rate of exchange for every engagement, only on average.

It is worth noting that attrition occurs naturally in war whether or not one's formations are actually involved in combat. Material and personnel losses take place routinely, indeed, almost daily, even in peacetime, though usually not at a rate as high as in wartime. Weapons and troops are lost not only through combat, but also due to accidents or operational wear and tear. In a single month during the Battle of Britain, the Fighter Command of the Royal Air Force (RAF) lost a third of its aircraft to a combination of friendly fire and accidents. As some historians noted, Fighter Command's losses through accidents alone would have been enough to bring about its demise by the end of 1940, but for a steady flow of replacements.

Likewise, from 1941 to 1942 the Japanese military reported 40 percent of its aircraft losses were caused by direct combat, while the remaining 60 percent were the result of training or transportation-related causes, such as accidents, sabotage, or the interdiction of transport. The basic operational lifespan for combat aircraft was three months, four months for tanks, and five months for artillery. For instance, the Soviet Red Army had to replace about 20 percent of its heavy equipment on a monthly basis simply due to operational wear and tear.

Militaries also routinely lose personnel through noncombat causes such as disease, desertion, or expiration of enlistments.

Historically, disease has eroded the fighting strength of armies or navies much faster than direct combat. Whether the cause is enemy action or routine consumption, militaries must replace their losses to preserve combat power. That requirement, in turn, makes maintaining their lines of supply critical. In its simplest terms, combat power is a subset of military power; it is the ability to perform in battle, and it is a function of numbers and proficiency, that is, quantity and quality. Replacing raw numbers lost in battle, while necessary, is never sufficient. Replacements usually do not immediately restore combat proficiency, since recruits need time to learn how to perform their tasks to the level of seasoned veterans. This fact was clearly demonstrated during the battle for the Philippine Sea in June 1944, when U.S. aircrews shot down their Japanese counterparts at a ratio of 5 to 1 largely because the former had more experience, better training, and a slight technological edge.

An increase in raw numbers can actually conceal a real decline in combat power. By January 1944, for instance, the Third Reich had lost nearly 4.2 million combat troops; however, it had conscripted enough replacements to boast of having almost 9.5 million personnel under arms. Yet, the ages of many conscripts fell outside the optimum range for military service (18 to 25); many others were involuntarily impressed into service with the Wehrmacht from Nazi-occupied territories, which meant their motivation was not high. Also, by this point in the war, German units were often understaffed in terms of experienced officers and noncommissioned officers (some having been promoted to fill vacancies at higher levels), which, in turn, impaired combat performance and led to higher casualty rates.

What's more, not all losses are equal. Neutralizing command centers can degrade combat power faster than destroying tanks and aircraft. During the Battle of Britain, the potential loss of radar (radio detection and ranging) stations—the "eyes and ears" of the RAF's Fighter Command—would have proved more hurtful than that of aircraft and pilots. Radar was not necessarily the "war winner" most postwar myths made it out to be, but it performed a critical service in an integrated system of air defense. Without its "eyes and ears," Fighter Command could not have concentrated its resources as efficiently as it did to counter the Luftwaffe's attacks. A loss in efficiency—especially in terms of managing fuel consumption and aircraft and pilot fatigue—would have resulted in a serious drop in effectiveness.

By 1944, German casualties in experienced pilots proved more damaging than losses in aircraft since more time was needed to train the former than to manufacture the latter. The shortage of trained pilots made the Luftwaffe's task of providing air cover for land and naval operations increasingly difficult, which, in turn, meant still higher casualty rates for the units conducting those operations. In short, casualties in certain capabilities and functions can lead to far-reaching second-and third-order effects and result in a precipitous drop in effectiveness. To replace their heavy losses at the front after 1943, for instance, the Germans had to draw more and more personnel from their labor force, replacing them with slave labor in some cases, which, in turn, adversely affected production.

The straightforward character of attrition suggests it can be reduced to a few simple equations. Perhaps the two most common of these belong to the British engineer and inventor Frederick Lanchester. At the height of the First World War, Lanchester developed two mathematical "power laws" or equations: the "linear law," which he said applied to classical warfare, and the "square law," which pertained to modern warfare. In classical warfare, Lanchester reasoned, each combatant typically fought only one opponent at a time, hence the linear law; whereas in modern warfare, crew-served weapons, such as machine guns, tanks, planes, and artillery, made it possible for combatants to engage multiple opponents simultaneously, hence the square law.

Lanchester's laws proved useful in the world of war gaming and in mapping branches and sequels for contingency planning. However, they were based too heavily on quantitative factors to serve as a reliable predictor of combat outcomes. Chance and qualitative factors, such as skill and morale, were too difficult to account for except by random distribution.

When the attack on the United States took place on December 7, 1941, Japan had 10 capital ships, 10 aircraft carriers, 38 cruisers, 112 destroyers, and 65 submarines. Against these, the United States and its allies had some 10 capital ships, 3 aircraft carriers, 44 cruisers, 93 destroyers, and 71 submarines. Of these, 5 U.S. capital ships, 3 cruisers, and 3 destroyers were either destroyed or heavily damaged at Pearl Harbor. Thus, that attack gave Japan a superiority of 2 to 1 in capital ships, 3 to 1 in aircraft carriers, but only roughly 1 to 1 in other categories. However, at the time, the United States had under construction a further 15 capital ships, 11 aircraft carriers, 54 cruisers, 191 destroyers, and 73 submarines. Production rates were subsequently accelerated for these vessels. As a result, U.S. admiral Harold R. Stark's remarks to the Japanese ambassador in 1941 would prove correct:

> While you may have your initial successes due to timing and surprise, the time will come when you will have your losses, but there will be this great difference. You will not only be unable to make up your losses but will grow weaker as time goes on; while on the other hand we will not only make up our losses but will grow stronger as time goes on. It is inevitable that we shall crush you before we are through with you.

Indeed, by war's end, the Allies had collectively out-produced the Axis by 3 to 1 in aircraft; 4 to 1 in tanks and self-propelled artillery; 7 to 1 in artillery pieces (mostly Soviet); and 2.5 to 1 in warships.

48,000 U.S. planes to 27,000 Axis aircraft; 25,000 U.S. tanks and self-propelled artillery to 11,000 Axis; and two U.S. warships for every one produced by the Axis. British and Soviet output extended the margin even further, adding 49,000 aircraft, 33,000 tanks, and 84 warships.

Murray and Millett, "Table 2: Major Weapons Produced by Allied and Axis Powers," *War to Be Won*, 252

For their part, the Japanese had anticipated the Allies would rebound materially. As Admiral Yamamoto said, "In the first six to twelve months of a war with the United States and Britain, I will run wild and win victory after victory... after that I have no expectations of success." However, the Japanese also had concluded that waiting for American and British military power in the Pacific to eclipse that of Japan was not an option; hence, the attack on Pearl Harbor constituted a desperate attempt to intimidate American leaders or, failing that, to weaken U.S. military power enough to give Tokyo time to conquer resource-rich islands, such as Borneo and Java, and to establish a formidable defensive perimeter. Japanese leaders estimated they had sufficient combat power to hold that perimeter, or at least to make advancing against it prohibitively costly for the Allies. Obviously, they had egregiously miscalculated.

While attrition is straightforward, carrying it out is not necessarily so. The strategy of the Allies in the Second World War was complex and multilayered. Manufacturing vast quantities of military hardware, mobilizing millions of personnel, and disrupting the production of Axis combat power and its flow to the front lines accounted for only a portion of the Allies' strategy of attrition. From the standpoint of practical execution, the strategy also required containing Axis advances, then progressively closing the ring ever tighter around Italy, Germany, and Japan. That meant coordinating the planning and timing of campaigns to ensure Axis forces were always fighting at a disadvantage, and that their shortfalls would grow increasingly worse with time. The vast territory the Axis powers had conquered became a double-edged sword because they lacked the resources to hold it, and their attempts to relocate reserves to crisis areas left them exposed to greater transportation-related attrition as well as the ravages of Allied air power. With a smaller area to defend, the Axis might have had better odds of inflicting prohibitive casualties on the Allies and possibly arriving at terms short of unconditional surrender. As it was, the aim of unconditional surrender was announced after the Casablanca Conference in early 1943; however, it is not clear whether it actually inspired German and Japanese troops to fight harder.

Exhaustion

Exhaustion can be thought of as a form of psychological attrition. It hits emotional or intangible factors such as morale and public confidence. Although such factors are by definition difficult to measure, they relate to whether an opponent believes further military action is likely to improve the prospects of victory. An adversary's political parties are likely to have conflicting views over how much a given war aim is worth, and that tension can sometimes be exploited. Exhaustion can manifest itself as quietly as a head of state's decision to withdraw from a conflict prematurely or as broadly as an increase in antiwar protests and a substantial drop in public confidence. Loss of public support for a war will likely have more to do with perception than reality, and it can occur even as one's military presence in a theater is growing and the situation in the combat zone is improving. U.S. forces in Vietnam gradually increased from 200,000 troops at the end of 1965 to more than 500,000 by 1968. However, American support for the war steadily declined over the same period, dropping precipitously after the Communist Tet offensive in early 1968, even though the Communists were defeated.

In August 1965, a Gallup poll asked Americans whether direct involvement in the Vietnam War was a mistake: 61 percent answered no; however, this figure decreased to 49 percent by May 1966 and then to 44 percent by October 1967. By the end of that year, only 39 percent of Americans approved of the handling of the Vietnam conflict. This figure dropped to 26 percent after the Tet Offensive in early 1968.

Gallup Poll conducted August 27, 1965, to November 13, 2000, http://institution.gallup.com.

Exhaustion can leverage all the advantages of the defense. As military theorist Carl von Clausewitz observed, the attacker's task is inherently more difficult than the defender's. The defender need merely to survive and to make the attacker grow weary of the struggle, while the attacker must subdue the defender. Thus, a strategy of exhaustion suits the basic nature of defense. When the tide turned in the Second World War, the Axis powers were essentially waging a war of exhaustion. If they could manage to win enough battles and inflict enough casualties, they might have prolonged the conflict and undermined the morale of the Allies.

Prolonging the war also might have allowed time for Germany to improve its so-called *Wunderwaffe* (wonder weapons), such as the V-1 and V-2 rockets and Me 262 jet aircraft. However, the growing material superiority and increasing operational skill of Allied forces denied the Axis the victories it needed; Allied ground offensives deprived Germany of the time it required to produce its miracle weapons in numbers sufficient to turn the tide. Furthermore, the leaders of the Axis had miscalculated the resolve of the Allies, whom they saw as racially and psychologically inferior, and their frequent use of terror to weaken that resolve generally produced the opposite effect.

A strategy of exhaustion can take several forms. Among the most frequent are blockades, sieges, "scorched earth" policies that destroy land an attacker might use, or almost any approach, including guerrilla warfare, that typically involves trading space for time or avoiding decisive battles until one is ready. Blockades have been defined in various ways, and they can be used for purposes ranging from a quarantine against select items of contraband to cutting a party's overseas or overland communications. Those blockades designed to starve or undermine an adversary's civilian and military populations by reducing imports of food and other essentials are typical of a strategy of exhaustion. The object of a blockade is usually twofold: to reduce a party's ability to produce war materials and to bring its population to its knees by increasing the pain it must endure.

An example is the Royal Navy's blockade of Germany during the First World War, also known as the "Hunger Blockade." Historians debate how many Germans might have died from starvation as a result of it, but most estimates exceed 750,000 people. The blockade reduced German imports by more than 50 percent and cut off supplies of coal and fertilizer materials critical for agricultural production as well as vital food staples such as dairy products, grain, and potatoes. The Germans tried to compensate with *Ersatz* (substitute) food products such as composite bread and powdered milk, but these were greatly inferior in nutritional value. The low calorie count and lack of nutrition in German diets led to higher rates of disorders such as tuberculosis and dysentery. This type of blockade is also a form of economic warfare, and it can require months or even years to generate results. It is essentially a large-scale siege. Blockades can be used in wartime or peacetime, further illustrating how military strategy is not confined to situations in which the parties involved are in a state of overt war.

As alluded to above, a siege is like a cordon or naval blockade, but on a smaller scale. It usually is employed against a city or fortress too strong for the attacker to take outright. During the Second World War, Hitler ordered his divisions to besiege Leningrad (now St. Petersburg) rather than take it by storm because he thought an assault would be too costly. The siege that resulted lasted nearly 900 days from September 8, 1941, to January 27, 1944. More than 600,000 Russians are believed to have perished during it, though some estimates are closer to 1,000,000, in attempting to account for the tens of thousands of people who died but were never reported to authorities. Not only were food supplies cut, but also coal stores were depleted as the winter of 1941 approached, freezing pipes and denying fresh water to the residents of the city. Despite extreme levels of starvation and other privations, the city held until Russian forces liberated it in 1944.

In contrast, Dien Bien Phu (1954), a small outpost along the border between Laos and Vietnam, was a completely different kind of siege. In March and April 1954, nearly 40,000 Vietminh forces under General Vo Nguyen Giap systematically encircled some 13,000 French troops occupying the outpost. Nonetheless, French general Christian de la Croix de Castries believed he could keep his forces supplied by air, and he also saw the encirclement less as a danger than an opportunity since it brought his enemy within range of his artillery. However, French resupply efforts fell short in the face of relentless Vietminh assaults, and the defense of Dien Bien Phu collapsed on May 7, 1954, marking one of the most humiliating defeats in French military history. Hunger and disease are usually the attacker's allies during a siege, but in the case of Dien Bien Phu it was more a matter of combat systems and munitions. Such "allies" can prove fickle, nevertheless, and may bring ruin to any besieging force that is not prepared properly.

A "scorched earth" policy is the proverbial sword that cuts both ways. The Russians employed such policies successfully against their two major invaders of the modern era, Napoleon in 1812 and Hitler in 1941. Napoleon's Grande Armée had its own supply system, but it gained a large portion of what it needed by foraging the countryside through which it passed—taking crops, livestock, and water from the farms and villages it passed. Thus, Tsar Alexander's policy of scorched earth removed or destroyed much of what Napoleon's army needed to subsist on and exacerbated his supply problems. Stalin's scorched earth policy was a source of frustration for Hitler's army, which had not prepared adequately for the logistical challenges it would face traversing the vast distances of Russia or for the fierce Russian winter. A strategy of scorched earth also can have an offensive aspect, as Union general William T. Sherman demonstrated in his march on Atlanta (1864). His aim was to make the South, and Georgia in particular, feel the "hard hand of war" for seceding. His troops attempted to do this by looting crops and livestock, destroying railroads, and burning buildings; it was a combination of economic and psychological warfare that undermined Southern morale, increasing the economic hardships Southerners faced and showing that the Confederate army could not protect the home front. As always, civilians suffer most when such strategies are pursued, and they suffer by the hands of their own leaders perhaps more than those of the invaders. That is perhaps the chief disadvantage of a scorched-earth policy or a war of exhaustion in general.

Examples of guerrilla-style warfare include ambush and raiding, as carried out by General Nathanael Greene and Admiral John Paul Jones in the American War of Independence, Mao Zedong in the Chinese Civil War, and Ho Chi Minh the First and Second Indochina Wars. Other instances include the use of force in a more conventional sense, as Frederick the Great did in the Seven Years' War or as George Washington did in the American War of Independence. Of course, any of these methods might be combined as the situation requires.

Greene's tactics were essentially those of ambush, raiding, and sabotage; these were carried out both to frustrate the British and to influence local public opinion. Gaining influence was doubly

Attrition and exhaustion

41

important because historical evidence suggests only one-third of the American population at the time supported going to war against the British Crown, while one third remained loyal, and the remaining third was reluctant to commit to either. A psychological campaign was thus crucial to maintaining support for the Revolution and to winning over the uncommitted third. Greene's forces made use of the existing system of mills, the economic centers of the eighteenth century, to replenish their provisions and, whenever possible, deny replenishment to the British.

George Washington has been referred to as the "American Fabius," and even Greene described Washington's strategy as seeking to skirmish rather than to seek a decisive battle. However, unlike Fabius, Washington did engage in major battles against his more skilled foe; thus, he took far greater risks than did the Roman general. Washington was sometimes forced to offer battle because Congress urged him to do so in the naïve hope victory could be achieved in one swift engagement or because the British had maneuvered him into a tight position. At other times, he seems to have sought it as a matter of preference. His army initially consisted largely of militia and short-term volunteers, who lacked the discipline and training to go head to head with the British. Nonetheless, they could inflict considerable losses under the right conditions, and every British casualty was many times more difficult to replace than an American one. Thus, the necessary ingredients were present for Washington to inflict both physical and psychological harm on the British, as long as he could keep his army from being destroyed or dissolving from loss of heart.

Victories, even on a small scale, can be important for their psychological value. Victories strengthen resolve, offer proof of military prowess, and help attract allies and other forms of external support. This was as true for Washington's army as it was for Mao's revolutionary forces in the Chinese Civil War and for Ho Chi Minh's guerrillas, though the latter two also made liberal use of terror tactics as well as aggressive "strategic messaging" to control civilian populations.

Attrition and exhaustion remain the Achilles' heels of annihilation and dislocation. The latter strategies seek quick decisions; the former turn that aim into a vulnerability by prolonging the conflict. Attrition works best when used against materially weaker foes; exhaustion can help inferior powers outlast materially stronger ones, even when they are using attrition. However, one must have the requisite political and cultural patience to employ these strategies. Some political causes, such as "national liberation," are more tolerant of prolonged military campaigns and high casualties than others. The West's cultural sensitivity to casualties has varied historically. Whatever the reason, sensitivity to casualties can make either type of strategy infeasible. Some military experts eschew such strategies for their lack of imagination and typically high costs, but they can be very effective in breaking an opponent. Moreover, one may have to consider resorting to attrition or exhaustion if one's initial plans fail.

Attrition requires appropriate metrics for keeping track of how much of an opponent's combat power has been destroyed compared to how much is being produced; with exhaustion such physical measures are less important, but gauging the morale and confidence of an adversary is critical to sound decision making. Unfortunately, even with modern sensors and information technologies, it is difficult to assess battle damage accurately. Combatants often go to great lengths to conceal the extent of the harm done to them. Damaged vehicles and equipment will be repaired; dead or wounded soldiers will be buried or removed to prevent an accurate count of personnel losses. One of the most egregious examples of casualty inflation is the "body-count syndrome" of the Vietnam War. American leadership made body counts an important criterion for measuring success in Vietnam, which encouraged commanders to inflate their reports of enemy casualties, which, in turn, led to inaccurate assessments of progress and unrealistic expectations. In fact, as several military critics noted, in some cases, on-the-ground assessments were not conducted at all: in 1968, for instance, only 13.5 percent of B-52 strikes were followed by on-the-ground evaluations.

Likewise, both British and German reports of aircraft shot down during the Battle of Britain in 1940 were inflated nearly twofold. (The RAF claimed roughly 2,700 kills, but the Luftwaffe's actual losses were closer to 1,700. The Luftwaffe claimed 3,200 kills, but RAF losses were nearer to 1,600.) Fortunately for the British, they overestimated the strength of the Luftwaffe at the beginning of the campaign, whereas the Germans had underestimated the initial strength of the Royal Air Force. Hence, as the battle progressed the Luftwaffe thought it was closer to breaking the RAF than it actually was and, as a result, took greater risks. With respect to the progress of the war overall, the Allies overcame ambiguities in their statistical measures partly by maintaining relentless pressure on the Axis via conventional land campaigns. They were able to measure progress in terms of not only hardware destroyed or personnel casualties inflicted, but also by the advance of their forces over Axis-held territory. That variable for measuring progress was not available in the Vietnam conflict; other measures, such as counting numbers of villages freed and of South Vietnamese forces trained, were often tentative at best.

Attrition and exhaustion require time to work, and any interval of time affords one's opponent an opportunity to develop countermeasures, whether those take the form of new resources, stronger allies, or better strategic techniques. In the Second World War, the Allies needed time to build combat power; but they had to do so before some members among them, namely, the Soviet Union and China, were driven to surrender, or the Axis itself simply grew too strong. Even after the tide of the war turned in favor of the Allies, the Third Reich continued to search for superior tanks, aircraft, and rockets capable of making the war too costly for the Allies.

In effect, the relentless Allied advance deprived the Axis of territories from which it could draw valuable manpower and other resources. It also put unremitting pressure on the Axis leadership, causing it to commit newly outfitted replacement formations prematurely, or in suboptimal ways. The Axis powers simply lacked sufficient resources to enable them to overcome such pressures and to recover from their blunders. Fortunately for the Allies, the material superiority they enjoyed enabled them to recover from most of their strategic errors. One such error was the invasion of mainland Italy in 1943, which, according to many observers, had seemed a good idea at the time due to the collapse of Italy's Fascist party and the promise of more airfields for Allied planes. But the Italian campaign proved difficult and costly.

Of course, geography and terrain also can influence the odds of success for either attrition or exhaustion. The U.S. military found it difficult to apply a strategy of attrition during the Vietnam conflict not only because the NVA (North Vietnamese Army) and Viet Cong took advantage of the thick jungle vegetation to conceal their movements, but also because the "political" geography of the region afforded them safe havens in Cambodia and Laos to which they could withdraw to rearm and reconstitute. Likewise, Pakistan became something of a safe haven for al Qaeda and Taliban forces during Operation Enduring Freedom in Afghanistan. Had the physical and political geographies of Vietnam and Afghanistan been similar to that of the Korean Peninsula, where a defensible demilitarized zone could be established, a strategy of attrition in conjunction with "clear-hold-and-build" operations might have succeeded against the opponents' strategies of exhaustion.

Employing strategies of attrition or exhaustion generally will require taking the following considerations into account. First, one needs to assess how one's resolve compares to that of one's opponent with respect to the stakes at hand. Second, one must determine the degree to which material strength alone could prove decisive. Third, one has to evaluate how physical and

Chapter 4
Deterrence and compellence

The Roman military writer Publius Flavius Vegetius Renatus once wrote, *"Igitur qui desiderat pacem, praeparet bellum"* (Let whoever desires peace prepare for war). To ensure peace, in other words, we must prepare for its opposite. The sentence is as ironic as it is memorable. Vegetius's axiom is surely a warning based on a realist's view of human nature. However, it also underscores the core principle of deterrence: to discourage aggression, we must appear strong enough to defeat an attack, or at least to make it too costly to be worthwhile. To be sure, preparing for war is not necessarily the best way to secure peace. Arming ourselves can inspire fear and mistrust among our neighbors and possibly lead to a preemptive strike, in effect causing what we sought to avoid. On the other hand, if we appear weak or unprepared for war, we might invite aggression. The line between deterring an attack and provoking one can be thin indeed. By way of illustration, in 1912 France and Russia had begun to outpace Germany in the arms race then under way; that fact added to Germany's growing sense of insecurity, and it contributed to Berlin's decision to go to war in 1914 rather than to allow the military situation to deteriorate further.

We can discuss the military strategies of deterrence and compellence together because one is in effect the inverse of the other. Deterrence is commonly defined as making people decide *not* to do something, such as launch an attack. Compellence, a term invented by the economist and Nobel Laureate Thomas Schelling because he believed the English language did not have a counterweight to deterrence, is usually understood to mean forcing people *to do* something, such as withdraw their military forces. Deterring or dissuading someone from doing something usually requires some form of compellence as well. Similarly, forcing someone to do something typically means carrying out more than a few deterrent activities.

Both military strategies fall within the broader category of strategic coercion, and they focus on reducing an opponent's willingness to fight rather than its material capacity to do so. However, each strategy can achieve that aim by creating a material imbalance short of going to war, either by eliminating some of an adversary's capabilities or by producing more of your own.

Nonetheless, such an imbalance, however formidable, has little coercive value unless it is accompanied by the political will to use it. Yet determining whether the willingness to use military force exists is ultimately a subjective call. In 1936 Hitler realized Britain and France were much stronger militarily than Germany, but he predicted, rightly, they would not respond with military force if he sent his troops to reoccupy the Rhineland. Had either Britain or France reacted, Hitler later admitted, "we would have withdrawn with our tails between our legs." At that time, however, neither the French nor the British had the political will to force the issue.

Some experts distinguish between coercion conducted short of war—with activities such as mobilizing military forces, initiating training exercises along a border, or conducting aircraft overflights—and coercion during war. The former is sometimes referred to as "coercive diplomacy" or "armed diplomacy" or "forceful persuasion." Hitler's desire for expansion juxtaposed against the desire for peace by Britain and France made his use of coercive diplomacy between 1936 and 1939 quite effective. His style of coercive diplomacy combined elements of deterrence and compellence; the idea of going to war, even with favorable odds, was unpleasant enough to British and French diplomats such that Hitler could use it to both compel their acquiescence and deter them from taking military action.

For some military theorists, such as Clausewitz, compellence—or the use of violence to force an opponent to do one's will—is the basic purpose of war. But his concept of war also included putting foes in positions where they could not do anything but comply because they were powerless; hence, his full definition implies deterrence by denial. Since diplomacy does not cease when war begins, and since some uses of force, such as aircraft overflights, can be considered acts of war, it can be difficult to draw sharp distinctions between coercive diplomacy, compellence, and other forms of coercion. This is especially true when the employment of military force occurs in peacetime, or more precisely in situations once referred to in defense circles as "military operations other than war." Such operations typically include enforcement of sanctions, implementation of no-fly zones, counter-drug operations, and strikes and raids. The use of military force in such operations might still qualify as coercive diplomacy because sometimes the threat of force must become actual force to establish credibility or to demonstrate resolve.

Deterrence

To deter means simply to discourage or dissuade. A military strategy of deterrence amounts to making our adversary believe we have the physical and psychological capacity either to defeat an act of aggression or to make its costs exceed its benefits. Experts generally recognize four types of deterrence: *direct*, which refers to deterring an attack against oneself; *extended*, or deterring an attack against a friend or ally; *general*, or deterring a potential threat; and *immediate*, which refers to deterring an imminent attack. Both Pakistan and India are practicing direct deterrence since each maintains military forces capable of dissuading aggressive acts by the other, though several wars, border incidents, and skirmishes between the two powers have made the state of deterrence imperfect and tentative. Since July 27, 1953, UN military forces have fulfilled an extended deterrence mission along the demilitarized zone (DMZ) on the Korean Peninsula, though again there have been numerous clashes and border incidents. As a negative example, French and British efforts at immediate and extended deterrence on behalf of Poland failed to convince Hitler not to invade that country on September 1, 1939.

During the Cold War, the study of deterrence theories expanded enormously, and virtually every type of deterrence was employed in some fashion by the superpowers or their allies. Given the destructive power of nuclear weapons, preventing their use—whether as part of a general war or otherwise—became the concern of most deterrence theory. Nuclear deterrence hinged on maintaining a "balance of terror," meaning an attack by any party could result not only in defeat, but also annihilation, which could extend to allies as well as neutral parties. For that reason, in 1946 the renowned strategist Bernard Brodie called into question the utility of the atom bomb—the "absolute weapon"—as a political instrument. Brodie believed nuclear weapons had created a revolution in strategy because it made only two political objectives rational: the avoidance of armed conflict or its containment.

Nonetheless, within a few years nuclear weapons had become integral to U.S. president Dwight Eisenhower's policy of "massive retaliation," which promised to answer any act of aggression with enough military force to destroy the aggressor. The Eisenhower administration formally announced the policy in 1954, but it was too inflexible to endure long. Using nuclear weapons against an all-out invasion of one's homeland, or that of an ally, might be justifiable, but employing them against a minor power engaged in a local conflict would have been seen as excessive, perhaps even immoral.

As a consequence, nuclear weapons would be referred to by some political leaders, such as Mao Zedong, as a "paper tiger." Indeed, the conflicts in Korea and Vietnam seemed to prove Mao's point; Brodie's absolute weapon neither prevented nor contained the spread of conflicts associated with revolutionary movements. That point notwithstanding, Mao's views did change once he came to appreciate the value of nuclear weapons in deterring both the United States and the Soviet Union from attacking each other directly.

Although the balance of terror did not bring about the revolution in strategy Brodie described, it did create a new strategic reality and a novel challenge for deterrence theorists. The United States and the Soviet Union eventually settled into a deterrence policy of mutual assured destruction, or MAD (the irony of the acronym was lost on no one). The basic concept of MAD was that each party should possess sufficient second-strike capability to ensure the destruction of the other in the event of a surprise first strike. Yet for the policy to work both parties had to agree the other could possess a second-strike capability sufficient to cause assured destruction. Hence, as histories of U.S.-Soviet nuclear policies show, MAD quickly gave rise to mutual agreed assured destruction (MAAD). While the concept of mutual agreed assured destruction had its weaknesses, it underscored an important corollary for a strategy of deterrence, namely, mutual vulnerability could contribute to mutual security. In other words, if both parties truly desired peace, they would have to permit some degree of vulnerability within their defense postures.

By 1985, the United States possessed some 24,000 nuclear weapons and the Soviet Union owned about 40,000, not including chemical and biological munitions. Both sides eventually agreed to limit their nuclear stockpiles with the Strategic Arms Limitation Talks (SALT), and then to reduce them through the Strategic Arms Reduction Talks (START). By 2002, the United States and the former Soviet Union had

5. American paratroopers and Ukrainian mechanized troops work together in live-fire training exercises near Yavoriv, Ukraine, in January 2016. Combined training exercises of this sort contribute to deterrence by strengthening relationships among allies and coalition partners and by demonstrating resolve to would-be aggressors.

reduced their nuclear stockpiles to 11,000 weapons each. The balance of terror had held, and nuclear conflict had clearly been averted.

The Cold War ended in the early 1990s with the economic exhaustion and dissolution of the Soviet Union. That outcome inspired experts to claim, with some justification, that deterrence had succeeded. However, others challenged this view, insisting that while no major war took place between NATO and the Warsaw Pact, several peripheral or "brush-fire" wars broke out in Latin America, Asia, and the Middle East. The Cuban missile crisis in 1962 and the 1973 Arab-Israeli War, for instance, were crises that came very close to escalating. Critics also argued that the Reagan administration dangerously undermined deterrence in the 1980s by vastly increasing U.S. spending in conventional weapons, such as the Strategic Defense Initiative (also known as "Star Wars") and stealth technologies. Experts also wondered whether the West could learn from the mistakes it made during the Cold War and apply deterrence more effectively in the multipolar, post–Cold War environment.

Since the end of the Cold War, the United States, its allies, and the People's Republic of China have been practicing various kinds of deterrence in the Western Pacific region. Beijing has implemented a form of direct deterrence by positioning several hundred land-based, anti-ship ballistic and cruise missiles in a manner that could deny or restrict the movement of other countries' naval vessels within the East China Sea and the South China Sea. Beijing may well see this strategy as "counter-intervention" or "peripheral defense," since it is designed to prevent foreign powers from interfering in offshore areas the Chinese see as vital to their interests.

In the Pentagon's view, by contrast, this strategy is one of "anti-access/area-denial" (or A2AD) since it hampers the ability of the United States to provide extended deterrence for its allies in the region. Beijing's counter-intervention strategy includes not only the use of modern air and missile technologies, but also what the Chinese call "political warfare," which entails refuting the lawfulness of any interventionist acts (also known as law warfare or "lawfare"), the mobilization of public opinion against an intervention, and psychological warfare. In response, the United States and its allies have considered employing their own A2AD strategy, one that would restrict the movement of Chinese and North Korean vessels within the Western Pacific region. If implemented, the West's countermove will result in overlapping missile and aircraft defensive zones along the Pacific Rim.

Clearly, deterrence can succeed, but it has several important limitations. First, it can be difficult to assess how well a strategy of deterrence is working. It is not always possible to know whether the absence of armed conflict was because of deterrence or despite it. As Henry Kissinger, the former U.S. National Security Advisor, once noted, "Since deterrence can only be tested negatively, by events that do not take place, and since it is never possible to demonstrate why something has not occurred, it became especially difficult to assess whether the existing policy was the best possible policy or a just barely effective one."

The second limitation is deterrence's inherent fragility, which is closely related to its ambiguity. By the mid-1980s, it was not uncommon for experts to see deterrence as a gamble involving any number of shifting technological, military, political, and diplomatic variables.

For these reasons, it is unreasonable to expect deterrence to preserve peace over the long term unless both sides actively commit to avoiding war. Technological, military, political, and diplomatic power relationships will inevitably alter over time, sometimes dramatically, giving one party an opportunistic advantage over the other. In 1890, for instance, Britain held the lead in naval power (in terms of capital ships) with France and Russia in second and third place, respectively. By 1906, the situation had changed: Britain still held first place, but now the United States had moved into second, France had slid to third, Japan had moved into fourth, and Germany into fifth. By 1913, Britain continued to lead, but Germany had overtaken the United States for second place, while France and Japan had become tied for fourth. In short, the naval balance of power changed at least three times in the quarter century before the Great War, giving several nations relative advantages over their rivals and potentially opening the door to an armed conflict. It is useful, therefore, to think of deterrence not only as desired outcome, but also as a process requiring constant attention.

Third, as with any military strategy, successful deterrence depends on knowing one's adversaries, especially since not all would-be aggressors can be deterred. Some, like Adolf Hitler, can be delayed, but not truly deterred; if they pause, they do so only long enough to gain a better advantage. In addition, in the post–Cold War era, the phenomenon of so-called suicide bombers has challenged the traditional understanding of deterrence. The certainty of death, for instance, did not prevent the terror attacks of September 11, 2001, in the United States. If would-be attackers do not fear death, how can they be deterred?

Various theories have been advanced regarding how to deter fanatics and so-called irrational actors. These theories include using denial (hardening defenses, dispersing targets) to reduce the likelihood the attacks will achieve their desired effects (such as mass casualties), and the use of retaliatory strikes to ensure that the costs of such attacks are always high and are borne more broadly. Again, the success of such measures remains difficult to assess. This difficulty is further compounded when a marked dissimilarity exists in the respective values of each of the belligerents.

Fourth, perhaps more than any other type of military strategy, deterrence requires a similarity in outlook, or a baseline of expectations, from which each party can understand the actions and reactions of the other. One way to describe this similarity in outlook is by means of the term "rational actor." It can be defined in various ways, but in this context it means parties inclined to weigh the costs and benefits of military actions in a similar manner. Without such a basis, misunderstandings are likely to occur, which can lead to overreactions.

The theories of Herman Kahn, a defense analyst at the RAND Corporation, are examples of thinking that could be classified as outside the rational-actor model. Kahn rejected the conventional wisdom, which was held to be rational at the time, that nuclear war was suicidal. Instead, he dared to "think the unthinkable" and assume a nuclear exchange could be won. To support his argument, he developed a detailed escalation ladder consisting of 44 steps, the last of which was "Spasm" or "Insensate War." By this step each party's command centers have been destroyed, but they continue to launch their weapons reflexively, like a spider whose legs continue to twitch after it has died. According to Kahn, either side could choose not to escalate at any point along the ladder. However, his analysis downplayed the influences of fear, friction, culture, and psychology (though it acknowledged them), all of which would make it difficult to halt escalation once it has begun. By positing that nuclear war was winnable and by oversimplifying the dynamics of escalation, Kahn's theories required heads of state to accept undue risk in their strategic calculations; in short, any head of state who subscribed to those theories would have been acting "irrationally" in the eyes of most strategic thinkers at the time. Kahn's ideas thus won more acceptance in the transparent world of game theory than in the much foggier realm of international relations.

Finally, because deterrence rests on a delicate balance of power, it may be more vulnerable to friction and chance than other military strategies. By definition, accidents, whether large or small, happen despite (or because of) our efforts to avoid them. In the realm of strategy, it can be difficult to determine whether an accident was truly accidental; was the military aircraft that crossed another party's borders simply lost or was it on a special mission? How parties respond to accidents or unforeseen events can easily upset deterrence, particularly if efforts at communication are misperceived; this is especially true of nuclear deterrence. The destructive capability of nuclear weapons and the speed with which they can be delivered offer little room for error. Communication is, therefore, vital, but cultural and psychological filters can act like a form of friction and distort one's intended message. That is not to say ambiguity is never beneficial in strategy. Sometimes it can be useful to keep rivals guessing as to where one stands; ambiguity is, in fact, one of the principles underpinning the 1979 Taiwan Relations Act, which clearly stated that the United States did not support Taiwan independence, but also laid the groundwork for what official sources refer to as a "robust unofficial relationship" between the two parties.

Compellence

Much like deterrence, strategies of compellence typically include such measures as punishment, denial, intimidation, and reward, tools which have been used for centuries. Rome's legions fought many punitive actions designed to coerce opponents rather than to annihilate or enslave them. Punishment might have been severe in some cases, as it was designed to compel obedience and deter disobedience at the same time, but ultimately Rome wanted tribute, not ruins. Medieval wars, as well, often aimed at coercing foes through military actions designed to punish or deny, such as taking livestock, burning crops, or imposing levies. Despite the abundance of such conflicts throughout history, the vastly destructive wars of the industrial age and the advent of nuclear weapons made it necessary to rediscover compellence as a military strategy for situations short of all-out war.

In the 1950s and 1960s national security analyst and military veteran Robert E. Osgood became the first political scientist of his generation to explore how to use military power beyond explicitly crushing an adversary, as in the Second World War. His book, *Limited War: The Challenge to American Strategy*, first appeared in print in 1957. In it, Osgood defined the purpose of war as employing "force skillfully in order to exert the desired effect on an adversary's will along a continuous spectrum from diplomacy to crises short of war to an overt clash of arms." He believed the measured application of military force could modify an opponent's behavior. At the time, the idea was as ageless as it was revolutionary because coercion, as a form of violent bargaining, is as old as warfare; yet by the middle of the twentieth century, military practitioners such as General Douglas MacArthur believed the true aim of war should be decisive victory, which would, in turn, make bargaining much easier or perhaps even unnecessary. According to such thinking, bargaining meant one had failed to achieve a compelling victory.

Osgood also regarded diplomacy and war as a "continuous spectrum" rather than as discrete activities divided between political and military authorities. Although the spectrum of conflict is often partitioned for legal, doctrinal, or bureaucratic purposes, Osgood reminded policymakers and military professionals that these divisions are essentially artificial. Strategic coercion was, in short, the continuation of diplomacy by other means.

Soon after the publication of Osgood's *Limited War*, another important strategic theorist, the Harvard economist and Nobel Prize winner Thomas C. Schelling, achieved lasting recognition for his systematic exploration of the concept of coercion. Schelling published a path-breaking book on this topic, called *Arms and Influence*, in which he argued that military force could not only shape an adversary's behavior short of all-out war, but also it could be applied in controlled and measured ways to compel, intimidate, or deter. "The power to hurt," asserted Schelling, "is bargaining power. To exploit it is diplomacy— vicious diplomacy, but diplomacy." The object of coercion or vicious diplomacy, therefore, is to alter an opponent's behavior, without having one's own conduct modified too greatly in the process. Schelling regarded most armed clashes as "bargaining situations," and this view formed the foundation for the "bargaining model" of war, in which military power serves as a form of currency to be expended in a process of violent bartering. The problem with this theory was amply demonstrated in Vietnam because Hanoi was prepared to endure more pain than Washington could inflict. As a consequence, political leaders in Washington found it difficult to barter their way to an honorable peace.

The U.S. Army's campaigns against the Plains Indians of North America illustrate Schelling's vicious diplomacy in action. Between 1865 and 1890, the U.S. Army fought nearly 1,000 engagements against the Plains Indians, the larger aim of which was to compel them to relocate to territories considered less valuable by the U.S. government, but to do so without provoking public outcry over the blatant inhumanity of the program. The compellence aspect of the program was based on the proverbial carrots and sticks (rewards and punishments) so characteristic of coercion; it consisted of positive incentives, such as offering food and shelter for relocating, and negative consequences for refusing to do so in the form of military force. The military element (the stick) concentrated on doing what armed forces have traditionally done in war—that is, attack an opponent's capacity to fight and to subsist. This strategy included a blend of attrition, exhaustion, terror, and divide and conquer approaches. The loss of shelter, food, ponies, and in some cases hostages, usually broke the will of the Indians to resist, particularly if such physical and psychological harm were inflicted during the harsh winters or summer droughts. Once the Indians' wherewithal was destroyed or taken, they had little choice but to comply with U.S. relocation policies. This brutal process of coercion—threats, negotiations, attacks, renegotiations, and renewed threats—was repeated time and again until the U.S. government achieved its aims.

Coercion theorists returned to the concept of compellence in the 1990s (they never left deterrence) when stealth and precision bombing technologies enhanced the potency of Western airpower. These technologies gave airpower greater flexibility as a coercive tool—one could hit an opponent quickly, precisely, and with much lower risk of friendly casualties. Contributions to coercion theory from this period attempted to take Schelling's ideas further. In the process, at least two schools of thought emerged. The first believes coercive strategies are most successful when threats need not be carried out; it is the threat of force, or pain yet to come, more than its actual use, or pain already inflicted, that is most important.

That was surely the case in 1994 when the United States threatened to intervene with military force to reverse a coup in Haiti; the threat was credible enough that no member of the Haitian junta that had overthrown President Jean-Bertrand Aristide opted to challenge it, and thus Aristide was restored to power. However, an even greater threat of force was not enough to compel Saddam Hussein into withdrawing his forces from Kuwait in 1990–91; Saddam's compliance was secured only through combat. What's more, limiting one's use of coercion to the threat of force runs the risk of overlooking just how common it is in virtually all wars—recall Clausewitz's definition of war as the use of force to compel an opponent to do one's will—save those aimed at genocide or extermination. Even ethnic cleansing, which differs in nature from genocide or the elimination of a group, involves coercing the group into removing itself from a territory.

Accordingly, the second school of thought views coercion (both compellence and deterrence) as a function of the threat of military failure, which typically involves the systematic destruction of an opponent's military capabilities until it realizes it would be better off if it complied. This is commonly known as deterrence by denial because at its core is the use of destruction to deny a party the ability to accomplish its aims, but it also applies to compellence. It was demonstrated in 1999 when NATO conducted a heavy bombing campaign against Serbian forces under President Slobodan Milošević. NATO's goal was to compel Serbian troops to withdraw from Kosovo, and the bombing campaign began systematically eliminating Milošević's military capabilities. Yet Milošević's decision to withdraw did not occur until June 3, 1999, more than seven weeks into the bombing campaign. By then, NATO leaders had publicly agreed to consider committing ground troops, the alliance had as yet shown no signs of cracking, and the Russians, who had previously backed the Serbs, had begun to cooperate with NATO. Amid such developments, Milošević's prospects for success dwindled. It was never clear whether there was any single move on NATO's part that induced Milošević to concede. Regardless, airpower and land power advocates debated afterward which of their respective military instruments was truly decisive in bringing about Milošević's decision. It may well have been neither; former U.S. National Security Advisor Zbigniew Brzezinski suggested it had to do more with Russian diplomatic pressure on Serbia.

Another notable success occurred in December 2003 when Libyan president Muammar Qaddhafi agreed to destroy his weapons of mass destruction and to open his program to Western inspection and verification. Again, pundits debated why Qaddhafi conceded. But long months of diplomatic pressure and economic sanctions as well as the threat of replicating the exercise of military force in Afghanistan in 2002 and Iraq in 2003 all likely contributed to his decision.

Both Kosovo in 1999 and Libya in 2003 illustrate how difficult it can be to determine which instrument of military power, if any, produced the truly decisive coercive effect against a foe, despite very strong arguments by the military services. The West's track record of successful applications of coercion, even with the potency of modern airpower, is mixed in any case. Accepting single-factor explanatory theories is always risky whether one is at peace or at war. Rather than attempting to sort through situational ambiguities to find *the* single most decisive coercive measure, if such exists, it is best to think of coercion as a compound employment of multiple forms of diplomatic, military, economic, and informational means. These means need not preclude the use of "carrots," such as the lifting of certain sanctions, even though doing so may run counter to some definitions of coercion. What matters in practice is not the definition; rather, it is whether the strategy can succeed.

Compellence has many of the same limitations as deterrence. It requires active monitoring of potentially fluid situations, credible communications across cultural and psychological boundaries, and at least some shared expectations as to certain actions. Like most other strategies, coercion is vulnerable to mirror-imaging, or projecting one's values and ways of thinking on to one's adversaries. Such projections lead to risky assumptions about what one's rivals hold dear and how they will behave. The American use of aerial bombing in the Vietnam War failed in part because of mirror-imaging; policymakers in Washington assumed Hanoi's leadership would respond to the bombing in the way they would have responded.

In theory, coercive diplomacy and other forms of strategic coercion offer more flexibility and greater control over escalation than military strategies such as attrition or annihilation. For instance, one can apply force in the form of "graduated pressure" to achieve limited gains, much like Moscow and Beijing have done in the second decade of the twenty-first century. One might first make a show of force as an implied threat, then apply force incrementally, such as by occupying select islands in the South China Seas; then one might increase the intensity or amount of force by adding troops or by increasing one's defensive measures in the vicinity until one's objectives are achieved. To stop the process, one's opponents have to use military force more assertively, which they might not be prepared to do. In this way, one can exert influence gradually, operating just under an adversary's escalation threshold. Theoretically, one could maintain the same approach once the shooting starts without necessarily committing more military power than necessary, or more than one's public will abide. However, in practice this gradualist method can backfire dangerously by giving one's foes the opportunity to seize the initiative, particularly if they do not feel the need to avoid escalation.

On the one hand, applying military pressure gradually or in stages offers the possibility of achieving one's objectives at minimal cost. On the other hand, it can also prolong a conflict, increase one's losses, and put one's objectives at risk, particularly when an administration presides over an indifferent, unwilling, or divided public. The influence of friction and human emotion can also make it difficult to measure and control the level of force one must employ. As the Johnson administration discovered, its gradualist methods in Vietnam resulted in incremental escalation in the hope that one more uptick in the level of violence would result in achieving U.S. aims. Yet it is unclear whether an American victory, or at least a favorable settlement, might have been achieved had the United States employed greater force at the outset; this option enjoyed only limited political support at the time.

In sum, deterrence and compellence constitute the proverbial opposite sides of the same coin. Making adversaries choose *not* to do something is closely related to making them elect to *do* something else. Both strategies require similar conditions for success: reliable knowledge of one's opponent, credible military power, active monitoring, and some shared communications and expectations. Without the latter two especially, both deterrence and compellence are vulnerable to unanticipated events. Certainly the conditions for success are not always present, and either strategy can lead to an arms race—which we may think of as an effort to keep pace with, or surpass, an adversary's military might. As history shows, arms races are often merely instruments of both deterrence and compellence.

Chapter 5
Terror and terrorism

"Terror is a psychological weapon of unbelievable power," claimed Jacques Soustelle, the governor general of Algeria during its bloody war of independence (1954–62). "Before the bodies of those whose throats have been cut and the grimacing faces of the mutilated," he continued, "all capacity for resistance lapses; the spring is broken." More than one million people lost their lives in the Algerian conflict, though terror was not the only weapon responsible. The use of terror typically takes one of two forms: either wholesale, indiscriminate bombing designed to break civilian morale, as with the strategic bombing campaigns of the Second World War, or selective, precise targeting, as with the political assassinations carried out by Algerian nationalists during their war of independence.

Terror and terrorism are military strategies largely because of their coercive power. They are used to break an opponent's willingness to fight or to induce a change in a rival power's policies or behavior. Terrorists usually choose their targets for psychological value rather than for material gain. In fact, a terror attack may cause little harm to a party's physical capacity to fight. Terror is not just a military strategy; criminal gangs and drug cartels often use it to protect their respective operations and to send warnings to their rivals. While the use of terror to coerce or intimidate may be as old as human society, it certainly appears more prevalent in the age of digital communications since the effects of every act of terror can reach a global audience the instant they occur.

If terror is little more than the use of violence to instill a crippling sense of fear, as Soustelle described, terrorism itself is more difficult to define. Official definitions of terrorism describe it as violence (discriminate or otherwise) directed against noncombatants to influence public opinion or to modify a government's policies. The U.S. Department of State, for instance, defines terrorism as "premeditated, politically motivated violence perpetrated against non-combatant targets by subnational groups or clandestine agents." However, as is often said, one person's terrorist is another person's freedom fighter. That was certainly true of Nelson Mandela, who became South Africa's first black president and helped abolish apartheid but not before being roundly condemned as a terrorist and enduring more than a quarter century as a political prisoner. Many militant groups— such as the Irish Republican Army (IRA), the Basque Homeland and Liberty (Euskadi Ta Askatasuna, or ETA), the Revolutionary Armed Forces of Colombia (Fuerzas Armadas Revolucionarias de Colombia, or FARC), and Hamas, Hezbollah, and al-Qaeda—have been identified as terrorist organizations, but of course they see themselves differently. In fact, distinguishing an act of terror from an act of resistance, or from an act of war, can depend almost entirely on one's point of view.

Some experts see terrorism as a tactic, a set of techniques, rather than a type of strategy. To be sure, in many cases that is true. Between 66 and 73 CE, the Jewish Sicarii (dagger-assassins) in Jerusalem killed high-profile religious and political figures who were thought to be loyal to the Romans. It was not just the assassinations, but the particular manner in which they occurred that caused terror and anxiety among the Jewish population: the Sicarii would approach their unsuspecting victims, perhaps while in a busy market square, inflict lethal wounds with concealed daggers, and then quickly melt back into the crowd. Such swift and brutal attacks created an air of terror that contributed to coercing portions of the population into supporting Jewish liberation from Roman rule.

However, experts also agree, when used systematically in pursuit of larger policy aims, terrorism can become a consistent and coherent strategy. At the 1972 Munich Olympics, for example, Palestinian terrorists killed 11 Israeli athletes. The massacre was purportedly part of a larger plan to bring the Palestinian cause onto the world's stage and, thereby, to force political change. One can find strategic uses of terror employed by several of history's revolutionary leaders, among them Vladimir Lenin, Mao Zedong, Ho Chi Minh, and Che Guevara. Many of them were to discover, however, that the use of terror can prove counterproductive because it can repel the very audience it seeks to attract.

Strategic terror bombing

Strategic bombing doctrine developed shortly after the First World War. It was shaped initially by the theories of an Italian army officer, Giulio Douhet, who in 1921 published an influential treatise, *Command of the Air*. American officers such as William "Billy" Mitchell and British officers such as Hugh Trenchard and John "Jack" Slessor also contributed ideas that advanced airpower doctrine during the interwar years. Mitchell was a signal officer in the U.S. Army who commanded American aviation units in France during the First World War. He published a number of works in the United States, most notably *Our Air Force: The Key to National Defense* (1921) and *Winged Defense: The Development and Possibilities of Modern Airpower—Economic and Military* (1925), each of these conveying essentially the same message as Douhet, namely, that modern warfare called for an independent air force capable of carrying out long-range bombing. Hugh Trenchard was the commander of the Royal Flying Corps during the First World War, and from 1919 to 1929 he served as chief of the Royal Air Force (RAF). Slessor was a fighter pilot in the Royal Flying Corps during the First World War who later served as the RAF's director of plans, and he helped develop its operational doctrine; his most important publication on air doctrine was *Airpower and Armies* (1936).

Douhet claimed one could terrorize a state into submission by bombing its "vital centers"—the social, political, economic, and military nodes essential to its functioning—thereby making a ground campaign redundant. Mitchell seconded these views, though he and other American airpower theorists at the time concerned themselves more with bombing industrial targets, such as armaments factories, rather than population centers; however, in many respects this was a distinction without a difference as factories and population centers were often in close proximity, and air power was not accurate enough to strike only factories. In any case, the underlying logic was that loss of morale would go hand in hand with the elimination of physical capability. Trenchard also favored the idea of bombing industrial centers; he saw the benefit in terms of not only disrupting production, but also as possibly breaking the morale of factory workers and, by extension, that of the general population. In his postwar report, Trenchard wrote, "At present, the moral effect of bombing stands undoubtedly to the material effect in a proportion of 20 to 1, and therefore it was necessary to create the greatest moral effect possible." As he went on to explain, the finite assets he possessed during the war could not destroy every major industrial center in Germany without prolonging the conflict for another four or five years. Instead, he focused on "attacking as many centres as could be reached, [and thus] the moral effect was first of all very much greater, as no town felt safe."

Although these early airpower advocates explicitly discussed striking industrial targets, the accuracy of aerial bombing was never sufficient to destroy those targets without causing massive collateral damage. Moreover, the goal of terrorizing the hostile populace was never truly absent from the discussion, and it was always at the very least implied.

Trenchard's ratio of 20 to 1 seemed high to critics at the time (and ever since), and it was unverifiable in any event. It was likely driven in part by his own experience with the bombings of London, as he was one of several commanders to offer a pessimistic outlook to the War Cabinet after the initial German attacks. It was also brought on partly by the low regard many officers and policymakers had for the "decaying" moral strength (psychological resilience) of the urbanized masses, which purportedly had grown more "nervous" and unstable after decades of enduring the enervating strains of modern conditions. In other words, if there was a weak link in a society's willingness to fight, many believed it was likely to be found among the underprivileged classes, who had already shown a tendency to band together in unions and to follow "antipatriotic" doctrines.

Terror bombing of this sort was explicitly mentioned as a possibility well before the Great War. In his *War in the Air* (1908), the British science fiction writer H. G. Wells predicted air bombardments would be terrifying, vastly destructive, and yet indecisive. By the next year, aviation experts in Europe and the United States readily warned how the great bombing planes of the future would prove to be veritable terrors. In fact, many claimed, the terror would reduce the likelihood of war in the long run. In 1912 General Helmuth von Moltke, chief of the German General Staff, had expressed high hopes for the results that might be achieved by launching air raids into the heart of Britain and France. Admiral Alfred von Tirpitz, chief of the German navy, agreed, but he expressed reservations about whether such bombing might provoke a moral backlash if bombs hit innocent children and the elderly. Perhaps if the destructive power were great enough, though, such concerns would disappear in the immensity of the bombing. Only months before the First World War began, aviators in America warned that air attacks against major cities such as New York could prove devastating given the likely loss of life from fire, high explosive bombs, and resulting panic.

Germany's dirigibles were better suited than fixed-wing aircraft for such long-range terror bombing since they could cruise at high altitudes and carry a heavier payload. All told, the Germans made 54 raids on London and other British cities during the First World War, and panic did spread as a result. Factory workers reportedly lost sleep from the stress, the media was in an uproar, debates in Parliament were heated, and British morale was said to be dipping. However, the challenges posed by weather and improved air defenses diminished the effectiveness of the zeppelins and other airships. In addition, once Britons proved to themselves they could survive such attacks, subsequent bombings became less terrifying. In short, a party's citizenry could rebound psychologically from the terror and shock of aerial bombing. The psychological effects of terror were thus not necessarily permanent.

None of that discouraged political and military leaders during the Second World War, however. Both Axis and Allied leaders attempted to win quickly by terror bombing each other's cities. Hitler's attempt to knock Britain out of the war in 1940 by bombing London and surrounding cities was the perhaps the most infamous instance. In the first two months of the "London Blitz," as it was called, nearly 20 missiles fell on London per day, causing great alarm and many casualties; but the blitz did not break British morale.

Later in the war, Hitler resorted to a new class of terror weapons, the so-called Vengeance weapons (V-1 bombs and V-2 rockets), in a desperate attempt to undermine British resolve and possibly rupture the alliance. From June 1944 through March 1945, some 2,500 V-1s and 1,000 V-2s rained down on London and nearby towns, killing 8,700 people and wounding thousands more; but, again, such terror from above failed to break Britain's willingness to fight. The Allies, too, tried terror bombing, partly in retaliation for Axis bombing campaigns, but also because many believed it could break German and Japanese morale and thereby bring about a speedier end to the war.

Strategic terror bombing assumes the will of a people and that of its leadership are linked. Accordingly, terrorizing the populace should drive the latter to capitulate. However, that did not happen in the Second World War, despite historically unprecedented destruction. The massive U.S. Strategic Bombing Survey, published after the war, attempted to explain why. One of its conclusions was that the morale of the Germans and Japanese did not break because they were under the harsh control of the state, which impeded the flow of information about the bombings and influenced public opinion through propaganda. Overlooked was the fact that strategic bombing against Britain, which was clearly not a police state, also had failed.

The survey's investigators calculated the Allies dropped approximately 1.3 million tons of bombs on German cities, which killed more than 300,000 people and wounded many hundreds of thousands more. The city of Hamburg alone lost more than 40,000 people within a few days in late July 1943; similarly, the use of incendiary bombs produced as many as 80,000 casualties in Dresden in February 1945. The city of Tokyo was also repeatedly bombed, the most devastating raid of which is believed to have caused 125,000 casualties in March 1945. During the course of the Pacific war, nearly 161,000 tons of bombs were dropped on the Japanese home islands. However, the U.S. Strategic Bombing Survey, published after the war, estimated that fewer than 10 percent actually hit their targets.

The Japanese finally surrendered in August 1945, but not before the United States had dropped two atomic bombs, one each on Hiroshima and Nagasaki, causing some 220,000 total casualties.

The degree to which these attacks actually influenced Japan's decision to surrender remains a matter of fierce debate, especially since the Allies had already destroyed some 40 percent of Japan's largest urban areas and had inflicted 2.2 million casualties, of which 900,000 were fatalities. In other words, the atomic bombs added a further 10 percent to an already appallingly high total number of casualties. Nor was it clear whether Japanese officials had sufficient time to assess the damage caused by the first attack before the second one was launched.

Despite such unclear results, advocates of strategic bombing remained convinced it could win wars, or at least shorten them, if the right targets could be struck, and with sufficient frequency. However, strategic bombing also was tried during the Vietnam conflict, although to little avail. Hanoi and other cities were repeatedly pounded from the air in an effort to bring North Vietnamese leaders to the negotiating table. American bombing rose steadily, from 63,000 tons in 1963 to 643,000 tons by 1968, a tenfold increase in five years. North Vietnam's manufacturing capacity was disrupted for a time, but its facilities were dismantled and relocated to other areas. The White House also had to deal with a growing moral backlash—as bombing levels rose, the antiwar movement intensified at home, and U.S. allies began to waver in their support of American direction of the war.

In the 1970s and 1980s the advent of "smart bombs" and other precision munitions greatly increased the accuracy of air strikes, and they offered the possibility of collapsing a state's will to resist while avoiding the horrific civilian casualties and vast devastation characteristic of previous strategic bombing campaigns. Accordingly, new air power theories emerged, such as "Shock and Awe," based on modifying an adversary's behavior through the pinpoint use of terror. American air commanders put the theory into action in Iraq in 2003 with a massive strike of combat aircraft and cruise missiles, the aim of which was either to decapitate the Iraqi leadership or, failing that, to terrorize it into submission.

Some U.S. officials predicted the Iraqis would awaken to find their country's political and military infrastructure shattered. However, such precision applications of terror proved less effective than expected, partly because the fear they inspired was only temporary and targeted populations simply waited out the storm.

Terrorism

By the middle of the twentieth century, it became possible for experts to refer to strategic bombing as "terror from above" and the attacks of revolutionaries and terrorist groups as "terrorism from below." Some of the most notable revolutionary leaders of the twentieth century initially saw terror as integral to their strategies for political change. Lenin openly advocated the use of "guerrilla warfare and mass terror" to coerce "the masses" psychologically and to defeat, if not exterminate, any counterrevolutionaries. Violent overthrow and control of the population through terror were key principles in Lenin's theory of revolution. Mao Zedong, too, promoted a theory of revolution in which the use of terror was essential to securing the support of the civilian population. "To put it bluntly," he said, "it was necessary to bring about a brief reign of terror in every rural area; otherwise one could never suppress the activities of the counter-revolutionaries." Mao's general theory consisted of three phases: creating and consolidating a political base of support among the population, expanding the base of support through progressively bolder attacks, and launching a full-scale counteroffensive. Clearly, support of the population was critical to all three. In what would become one of his signature sayings, Mao claimed, "The people are like water and the [Revolutionary] army is like fish." Without water, the fish simply die. Likewise, without the people's support, the revolutionary army dissolves. In early Maoist thought that support was to be secured by whatever means necessary.

In a similar sense, Ho Chi Minh also built his base of support in Vietnam largely through terror and psychological coercion. Minh's revolutionary forces, the Vietminh, attacked not only occupying troops—first Japanese, then French, then American—but also many Vietnamese civilians. By 1956, their successors, the Viet Cong, routinely used violence to intimidate Vietnamese villagers and to assassinate political leaders. Such actions sent clear warnings about where the population's political allegiances should lie. Between 1957 and 1960, the Viet Cong committed some 2,000 kidnappings and 1,700 assassinations. Sources at the time claimed this wholesale use of terror had essentially murdered "the cream of village officialdom," and created a pervasive sense of fear and insecurity among the Vietnamese people. This climate of terror further undermined the already dubious authority and legitimacy of the government of South Vietnam, which was perceived as corrupt, inept, and uninterested in protecting its citizens.

However, Mao and Che Guevara, among others, would eventually come to view the use of terror as a double-edged sword. In their view, the wholesale use of terror could prove egregiously counterproductive. In the late 1930s Mao's guerrilla forces faced a better-equipped Chinese nationalist army and a brutal Japanese invader; thus, they needed the support of the population for provisions and concealment. An indiscriminate use of terror during this period would have marked the Communist Red Army as no better than its opponents—the nationalists and Japanese—and perhaps lead to the betrayal and capture of some of its forces. As Mao said of his army's efforts in those years, it had been "70 percent expanding our own forces, 20 percent resisting the Guomindang [Nationalists], and 10 percent fighting Japan." Throughout the campaign against the Japanese, Mao's propaganda machine claimed responsibility for nearly every successful raid or ambush, whether conducted by his forces or not, and he accused his Nationalists allies of incompetence and corruption (some of which was true). By the time Japanese troops withdrew in late 1945, Mao's army had a relatively firm physical and psychological hold over many areas within China.

Initially a steadfast proponent of the use of terror, Che eventually came to believe it should be used only selectively. "Terror," he stressed, is "generally ineffective...since it often makes victims of innocent people and destroys a large number of lives that would be valuable to the revolution." At the same time, it could be used discriminately to "put to death some noted leader of the oppressing forces well known for his cruelty," or "for other qualities that make his elimination useful."

After Castro's successful overthrow of the Battista government in Cuba, Che attempted to export the revolution to other Latin American countries. His revolutionary model was based on using a cadre of hard-core revolutionaries (the *foco*) to agitate against the government and to create the conditions for an insurrection. As Che noted in his *Guerrilla Warfare*, Castro's successful revolution in Cuba offered three main lessons. First, popular forces can win a war against a regular army, despite an initial inferiority in numbers and equipment. Second, one need not wait for the conditions to be right before beginning a revolution because the insurrectionist *foco* can create them. Finally, in underdeveloped lands, such as Latin America, the armed struggle should be fought mostly in the countryside where the lack of communication and transportation networks would prevent government forces from quickly reinforcing one another.

Although Che's *foco* failed utterly in Bolivia in 1967 and led to his execution, it is illustrative as a method not least because its approach resembles that of the Zapatistas in southern Mexico and that of al-Qaeda in the Middle East in the early twenty-first century. In each of these cases, conditions were conducive for insurrection: tensions and discord were already present for such groups to exploit. In 1967 Che found the Bolivian peasants receptive but unresponsive. Moreover, the Bolivian communist party not only refused to assist him, it actively blocked his recruitment efforts. He and his *foco* thus became the equivalent of Mao's fish *without* water, and they ultimately succumbed because of it. Additionally, the rugged Bolivian countryside reduced the mobility of the *foco* considerably, rendering it vulnerable to the government's search-and-destroy tactics, aided by the Central Intelligence Agency (CIA) and other U.S. support.

In the meantime, counterrevolutionary theories also had recognized the importance of the populace. Military doctrine concerning counterinsurgency and counterterrorism began to refer to the necessity of "winning hearts and minds." This was a truly unfortunate phrase believed to have originated with British field marshal Sir Gerald Templar, who led a counterinsurgency campaign against guerrillas of the Malayan Communist Party during the "Malayan Emergency" of 1948–1960. The phrase had a range of meanings: from establishing or reestablishing an ideological bulwark against the spread of communist ideology in Malaya to encouraging the "undecided middle" of the population to collaborate with counterinsurgent forces. One should not take this slogan to be a recipe or formula for victory, though it has been repeatedly treated as such. Rather, it ought to be understood to mean that, for long-term success, counterinsurgency and counterterrorism require more than merely eliminating insurgents and terrorists. It also underscores terror's potential to do more harm than good by making one's opponent appear to be the lesser of two evils.

In fact, counterinsurgency theorists, such as the French officer David Galula, who served in the Algerian War, perceived immediately that the support of the population is essential for both insurgents and counterinsurgents. That was Galula's first law of counterinsurgency warfare. He developed three others. The first was that support is gained through an active minority; it is better to have a small base of support that is vocal and active than a large one that is silent and passive. Second, gaining the support of the population is contingent on achieving successes that demonstrate the will, means, and ability to win; it goes against human nature to support a cause that seems doomed to fail. Lastly, one needs to maintain an intensity of effort and have ready recourse to extensive means; counterinsurgencies are not for the uncommitted or indifferent, nor are they necessarily inexpensive. Galula added a number of lesser principles; these together with the laws mentioned above served as guidelines for counterinsurgency operations, the overall aim of which was to make the "water" uninhabitable for Mao's "fish."

In 1962 France lost its bid to retain Algeria. Nonetheless, Galula's laws and many of his principles became popular among those who advocated for greater counterinsurgency capabilities in modern military forces. However, such principles were all but forgotten in U.S. and NATO military doctrine in the years after the Vietnam War. The campaigns in Afghanistan and Iraq that occurred in the opening decades of the twenty-first century forced a rediscovery of counterinsurgency techniques. Unfortunately, counterinsurgency experts promised more than the techniques alone could deliver, which, in turn, led to unfulfilled expectations, a decline in public support, and a long and acrimonious debate in defense circles.

Modern experts consider insurgencies (and counterinsurgencies) not as types of strategies, per se, but as types of warfare, much like revolutionary warfare or partisan warfare. Belligerents in such wars might use strategies—ranging from decapitation, to attrition, to exhaustion, to terror or terrorism—either to overthrow or to strengthen a political regime.

Scholars may well continue to debate whether terrorism is a strategy or a tactic. Yet we may view terrorism not as specifically either, but as a strategic way or technique. In this sense, it constitutes an essential component in a larger strategy aimed at striking a government through its population. Terrorism can have any number of objectives, some of which will serve the terrorist group itself, some of which will manipulate or maintain control over the populace, and some of which will target the government. Such objectives might include coercing or enforcing obedience (intimidating), advertising, attrition or exhaustion (cost imposing), dislocation, provocation, outbidding, undermining security and stability (spoiling), and punishing. These objectives vary little from those any legitimate government might have, but their real importance lies in how they can facilitate linking terror tactics, such as bombings, assassinations, contamination of water or food supplies, and hostage-taking, to an organization's overall aims, such as regime change, territorial change, a revision of policy, or even maintaining the status quo. The basic point of using terror is to cause fear and then to leverage that fear to achieve one's goals.

In contrast to the revolutionary movements discussed earlier, some terrorist groups have sought territorial change rather than regime change. Instead of taking control of a state through revolution and attempting to reorient its entire political, social, and military structures, these groups sought to provoke a government to grant them independence or at least greater autonomy. Thus, they also needed to attract public support, not alienate it, and tended to use violence more selectively, limiting their targets to specific political, cultural, or military icons. In some cases, terrorist groups might target civilians in order to blame their rivals for the attack or to provoke a disproportionate response by the government. In any event, violence is too blunt an instrument for terrorists or counterterrorists to employ error-free for any length of time; terrorist attacks will provoke outcry and revulsion among the public, but so will retaliatory measures. Hence, the balance between terror and counterterror can be a precarious one.

A new terrorism?

By the last quarter of the twentieth century, many terrorist groups had grown dissatisfied with selective targeting. In their eyes, it seemed to have failed, and so they sought instead to obtain more visibility and leverage by causing greater casualties and thus creating a general atmosphere of terror. As a result, experts have come to classify terrorist groups, broadly speaking, as "traditional" and "new." Traditional terrorist groups include the ETA, FARC, IRA, and others. In contrast, the new generation of terrorists—typified by al-Qaeda and like-minded jihadist groups—has adapted to the forces of globalization and leveraged them to build international networks and transnational capabilities. Their organizations increasingly include members from the migrant and diaspora communities, and they have become more multinational and multiethnic than the so-called traditional terrorist groups. The new terrorism is driven by political aims of a nature and scale reminiscent of the revolutionary movements of the twentieth century; many contemporary terrorist groups seek regime change. They have subsequently turned to inflicting maximum casualties through indiscriminant bombing and the use of ever more powerful explosive devices. The logic driving them seems to be if 11 deaths can make 500 million people aware, as with the Munich massacre in 1972, then 110 deaths will achieve more, and 1,100 deaths even more. The purpose of such escalation is not merely to cow the opposition into granting concessions, but rather to weaken it, to undermine it by exposing its vulnerabilities, and, as far as possible, to reduce or negate its influence, perhaps ultimately destroying it.

On the other hand, even what many experts regard as the bloodiest terrorist organization of the twentieth century, Peru's Shining Path (Sendero Luminoso) has not killed as many people in its 20-year campaign of violence as traffic accidents have taken on U.S. highways or as many lives as terminal diseases, such as cancer, have claimed over the same period. The Shining Path is believed to have killed some 69,000 people over two decades, a tragic number. However, in 2003, a total of 42,643 traffic fatalities occurred in the United States alone. Added to this toll, some 585,720 people died of cancer in the United States in 2014; that number would equate to more than 10 million people over a 20-year period. Dealing with terrorism, in other words, requires a sober perspective so as to

6. Passengers in the New York City subway are warned to stay alert and to observe anything out of the ordinary that might indicate an imminent terrorist attack. This is one of many such warning signs to appear in public places after 9/11, and it illustrates how terrorism can alter fundamental aspects of everyday life.

avoid political and social overreaction; the effects of terrorism are obviously more dangerous than mere statistics might suggest especially because they can provoke negative political change and exacerbate social divisions.

Jacques Soustelle described terror, correctly, as a psychological weapon of unbelievable power. However, that weapon cuts both ways. Terror can indeed cause the "spring to break," but it also can cause it to recoil. Nations and groups can recover from the psychological trauma of terror tactics more quickly than attackers might expect. Moreover, attempting to bomb an opponent into submission also can prove damaging to an administration's image at home and abroad. Considered historically, "terror from above" (or strategic terror bombing) has failed to live up to expectations. Nonetheless, it is likely to remain an attractive option for modern states because it offers a way to take some kind of immediate action while also limiting one's liability and reducing one's risks. That might satisfy the public's demand for action in the short term, or until the next crisis.

Considered objectively, strategies of "terror from below" have proven more effective at achieving negative aims rather than positive ones. Negative aims include preventing contentious factions from uniting, sabotaging already tentative peace talks, convincing a wavering coalition member to withdraw rather than to stay the course, psychologically coercing a population to support a cause, or attracting additional fighters through headline-grabbing attacks. Positive aims, such as obtaining international support for claims of legitimacy, winning over neutral parties, or establishing a foundation for long-term stability, are much more difficult, since terror triggers not just fear but revulsion and antipathy. Such emotions can unite populations against a cause and deplete its well of support. In short, terror may indeed raise public awareness of a cause, but, at the same time, it may strengthen the public's determination to see that cause fail.

Chapter 6
Decapitation and targeted killing

In his timeless but controversial masterpiece, *The Prince*, the sixteenth-century political writer Niccoló Machiavelli warned his readers: "It is simply not sufficient to kill the ruler and his close relatives, for the rest of the nobility will survive to provide leadership for new insurrections." His words ring true even today, underscoring as they do the basic vulnerabilities of two popular and closely related strategies: decapitation and targeted killing. These military strategies attack an adversary's willingness to fight and physical capacity to do so. However, both are vulnerable to assuming that removing a leader or specific individuals will solve the problem rather than making it worse; sometimes a great deal more time and effort is needed to achieve peace.

Both strategies have been used widely to combat terrorists and insurgents. Both attempt to be more precise and more discriminate in the way in which, and against whom, force is applied than other strategies. Both terms are so closely related that one is often taken for the other, though they actually differ in important respects. In colloquial terms, decapitation is sometimes referred to as "striking the head of the snake," which usually means one of two things: either the elimination of a group's leaders so as to cause it to collapse, or to degrade swiftly; or the forceful replacement of a hostile party's leaders with more amenable ones. So decapitation does not necessarily mean assassination. In fact, it sometimes yields better results if a group's leaders can be captured and "turned" rather than killed. Decapitation resembles a strategy of dislocation insofar as it can disorient an organization, at least temporarily, by removing or "converting" its leader.

In contrast, targeted killing—also known as "leadership targeting," "strategic assassination," or "targeted assassination"—is more akin to attrition. In brief, targeted killing is the systematic assassination of personnel belonging to a hostile group, and it is analogous to what former CIA counterterrorism expert Bruce Riedel has called "mowing the grass." "You've got to mow the lawn all the time," he advised; the "minute you stop mowing, the grass is going to grow back." Targeted killing uses assassination as its primary method, and it is typically what follows a failed decapitation strategy. A strategy of targeted killing might aspire to destroy a hostile group; but a lack of will or resources, or both, usually means the goal is more modest, perhaps only disrupting or decimating an organization to buy time. The individuals who are targeted are not always the highest ranking leaders, or what counterterrorism professionals call "high-value targets" (HVTs). In many cases, they are mid-level organizers, planners, or suppliers, rank-and-file fighters, or some combination of these.

The United Nations defines targeted killings as "premeditated acts of lethal force employed by states in times of peace or during armed conflict to eliminate specific individuals outside their custody." However, targeted killings are not conducted solely by states. They also can be carried out by violent nonstate actors such as terrorist groups, criminal gangs, and militias, or even individuals. The Mexican criminal syndicate Los Zetas (the Zs), for instance, used terror tactics to increase its influence throughout Mexico. This group purportedly began when

31 mercenaries and commandos, most with special forces training in the Mexican military, became assassins and bodyguards for a drug-trafficking organization known as the Gulf Cartel. The Zetas eventually split from the Gulf Cartel and formed their own illicit drug and human-trafficking organization, which at one point controlled more territory in Mexico than any other crime syndicate. They are well armed with state-of-the-art weaponry such as rocket-propelled grenades and assault rifles, and the original 31 members (many of whom have since been arrested or killed) were well trained. Some of the tactics employed by Zetas include car bombs, grenade attacks, ambushes, mass killings, and targeted assassinations of mayors, judges, and police officers; they often leave a signature "Z" carved in the bodies of their victims as a warning to rival gangs and to law enforcement officials.

The opening decades of the twenty-first century have seen an increased use of drone strikes, which, in turn, has heightened public awareness of decapitation and targeted killings. However, these strategies are hardly new. Alexander the Great used a modified version of decapitation at the battle of Gaugamela in 331 BCE; he attacked the center of the Persian army where its leader, Darius III, was positioned. Alexander's assault never reached Darius, but it caused him and his entourage to withdraw, which, in turn, created confusion in the Persian ranks and rendered them vulnerable to defeat in detail by Alexander's Macedonian hoplites.

Modern examples of decapitation include the capture of Abimeal Guzmán in 1992, the leader of Peru's terrorist group Shining Path (Sendero Luminoso). The Shining Path emerged as a Marxist revolutionary movement in the 1960s, and its goal was to overthrow the Peruvian government; its name derived from the motto of one of Peru's original Communist Parties: "Marxism-Leninism will open the shining path to revolution." By the 1980s, it was employing aggressive guerrilla tactics against Peruvian officials, and it had attracted some 10,000 followers.

Counterterrorism experts estimate that it has been responsible for killing at least 69,000 people from the 1980s to the early 2000s. Fortunately, Peruvian police captured and imprisoned Guzmán and several other Shining Path principals in 1992, which caused a leadership vacuum within the organization as no clear lines of succession had been drawn up. The Shining Path's activities declined sharply thereafter, it suffered a number of military defeats, and eventually it split into smaller, contentious factions. This state of decline and disorganization remained in effect for nearly a decade after Guzmán's capture, when signs of Shining Path's resurgence began to appear.

In a similar manner, the apprehension of Abdullah Öcalan in 1999, one of the founders of the Kurdistan Worker's Party (PKK), led to the group's rapid, if temporary, decline. Öcalan helped form the PKK in Turkey in 1978 with the goal of establishing an independent Kurdish state, an idea the Turkish government refused to entertain. The PKK employed terrorist methods— kidnappings, assassinations, suicide bombings, ambush, and sabotage—in its bid to achieve an independent Kurdistan; some 40,000 people (Turks and Kurds, military personnel and civilians) are believed to have been killed as a result of PKK actions, many sanctioned by Öcalan. In 1999 Turkish authorities captured and imprisoned Öcalan, which prompted a cease-fire that lasted until 2004 when the PKK resumed its terrorist activities. In 2013 the imprisoned Öcalan issued a written statement declaring another cease-fire and calling for a withdrawal of PKK forces from Turkey. Undoubtedly, had Öcalan been killed instead of captured he simply would have become a martyr for Kurdish independence rather than being able to exercise a moderating influence on PKK activities.

Naturally, capturing hostile leaders is not always possible or desirable. Sometimes such leaders prefer to fight to the death or to kill themselves rather than surrender. At times, suspects are in locations that do not permit extradition. At other times, government officials may fear that bringing such figures to trial will only provoke more violence. That was certainly the case with the killing of al-Qaeda's principal leader, Osama bin Laden, in a raid on his Abbottabad, Pakistan, compound in 2011 by U.S. special forces.

However, in other cases states simply want to proceed with the systematic elimination of hostile or criminal leaders in the hopes their removal sends a warning to followers or potential imitators. Beijing, Moscow, and Washington have pursued such policies relentlessly for decades, despite vocal criticism about the lack of due process. Similar criticisms have long dogged Israel's targeting of militant leaders, one such case being the killing of Mahmoud al-Mabhouh, one of the purported leaders of the Palestinian terrorist group Hamas, in January 2010. Western officials and the international media have accused the Israeli intelligence agency, the Mossad, of tracking Mabhouh to a hotel in Dubai and murdering him there; Mabhouh was thought to have abducted and killed two Israeli soldiers in 1989, and his assassination might have been meant as both a retaliation and a warning.

Despite such examples of the increased employment of decapitation and targeted killing, they remain highly controversial strategic techniques. Some critics reject them as ineffective over the long term, and they also find them objectionable on legal and moral grounds. Yet effectiveness is a function of what one wants to achieve and how well one can measure whether it has been accomplished. An important point often obscured in the debate over effectiveness is the use by critics of arbitrary metrics to define success. Some describe success as a marked decline in the number of terrorist attacks or as a specific interval of terrorist inactivity. However, such statistics may have little to do with the aims of those policymakers and practitioners actually involved in developing and implementing a particular strategy. Success of any course of action must depend on what decision makers wanted to achieve, compared with the actual outcome (insofar as it can be known) and how expensive the strategy was to implement in terms of physical and moral capital. To assume otherwise is to obscure the issue.

Critics, academic and military, can rightly claim that neither decapitation nor targeted killing has worked in all cases. The foremost reason is that these strategies fail to address the root causes of a conflict, and they may make matters worse by perpetuating a vicious cycle of attack and reprisal. Indeed, some evidence suggests killing one insurgent often creates others who desire nothing more than to retaliate. Skeptics also can point to how easy it is for states to use (or abuse) decapitation and targeted killing without taking sufficient measures to limit collateral damage. Israel's assassination of the former Hamas leader Saleh Shehadeh in 2002, for instance, also resulted in the deaths of his wife and children, as well as dozens of casualties among others in the vicinity. It cast Israeli leadership in a negative light; the U.S. government and others roundly condemned the attack as "heavy-handed" and detrimental to prospects for peace. In such cases, however, it is less the tool that is at fault than those who misuse it.

Most legal concerns have to do with ensuring that due process and accountability are preserved through the entire sequence of events from the selection of targets to the act of firing. Some legislation already has been enacted for such purposes. However, more may be needed. The targeted killings of al-Qaeda and Taliban leaders, for instance, were ruled legal under U.S. law, specifically the September 2001 Authorization to Use Military Force Act, passed shortly after 9/11. U.S. legal authorities also determined that such killings were in accord with international law under Article 51 of the UN Charter. Nevertheless, these legal instruments do not grant authority to extend targeted killings beyond those groups involved in 9/11. In the meantime, legislators and civil rights organizations such as the American Civil Liberties Union (ACLU) continue to lobby for greater oversight of targeted killings in order to prevent overreach of executive powers.

The moral issues surrounding targeted killings are more complex. They turn on whether one believes assassinations can ever be morally justified. Broadly stated, Just War theory says a war must have a just cause, be a last resort, be declared by a proper authority, possess right intention, have a reasonable chance of success, and that its aim must be proportional to the means used. However, such conditions do not necessarily apply in cases not classified as war. If a state assassinates a criminal, for example, Just War principles would not apply. Also, the marked asymmetry in cultures or, more often, the outright rejection of any moral guidelines by one party in an effort to instill a paralyzing level of terror in the other raises the question of the universality of Western norms, such as Just War theory or its associated traditions. In addition, debates between consequentialists (those who justify a war act based on whether the consequences of not doing it are worse) and intrinsicists (those who believe certain acts are just or unjust in themselves) continue, and may do so for some time. Yet in some ways, the increased use of strategies of decapitation and targeted killing in the ongoing conflict against terrorists are forcing these two views into a new synthesis of sorts, one that may well update the Just War tradition even as it opens it to looser interpretations.

Decapitation

Such controversies notwithstanding, history suggests that decapitation works under certain conditions. For instance, the United States used it to break the back of the Filipino insurrection against the American annexation of the Philippines at the beginning of the twentieth century. Emilio Aguinaldo was the insurrection's key leader, and he was captured in March 1901 by American troops. U.S. authorities ultimately persuaded Aguinaldo to swear an oath of allegiance the United States, which he did in

April of that year, and quickly followed with a proclamation calling on all Filipinos to lay down their arms. Although some Filipino fighters continued to resist for another year or so, most followed Aguinaldo's urging and surrendered because his example carried such significant weight among the Filipinos, and his successors could not match his leadership and charisma. Had he been killed instead of persuaded to swear allegiance to the United States and call for an end to the fighting, he might well have become a martyr and inspired months if not years of further fighting. Again, it is sometimes more beneficial to capture hostile leaders rather than to kill them. Capture also proved important in the collapse of the Kurdistan Worker's Party and the Shining Path.

At other times, it may not be clear whether capturing is better than killing a hostile leader. Such was the case during the Haitian "Cacos" wars (1915–16 and 1918–20), when American forces captured some bandit leaders and killed those fighters who refused to surrender. Cacos were Haitian peasants who became guerrillas and mercenaries under the control of local warlords. As the bandit leaders were eliminated, the groups tended to dissolve since few peasants had the desire or skill to hold them together. At the same time, U.S. troops put into play a "guns-for-cash" program to encourage guerrillas to trade their weapons for money and amnesty; such incentives made holding the ill-disciplined groups together even more difficult. In this case, decapitation succeeded, but only as part of a two-pronged, top-and-bottom strategy: guerrilla leaders were pursued with violent means, while their followers were offered incentives to disarm. Nor was decapitation a long-term solution for securing U.S. political and economic interests in Haiti. Those interests required the United States to maintain military forces in Haiti capable of performing stability and support operations. In fact, the last U.S. troops did not withdraw from Haiti until 1934, some 18 years after the first Caco war began.

Decapitation also has proven effective when one's quarrel is with a head of state and not with the general population. Removing a head of state from power is referred typically to as "regime change," and at times, it can be accomplished with minimal bloodshed. In 1954, for instance, a CIA-backed coup forced Guatemalan president Jacobo Árbenz to step down. The CIA had fostered an information campaign that undermined the Guatemalan army's support for Árbenz; in fact, the army turned against him and threatened to depose him if he did not resign. In 1963 Washington and London cooperated in removing Prime Minister Cheddi Jagan of British Guiana by subjecting his country to an extended general strike and by altering its election system so that a coalition of minority parties won. In 1964 the White House supported a bloodless coup that ousted President João Goulart of Brazil. Much more controversial were the results of the 1973 coup that ended the presidency of Salvador Allende of Chile. The CIA helped create the conditions, or climate, for his removal. General Augusto Pinochet then seized power as a result of the coup. He subsequently presided over one of the most brutally repressive regimes in Chilean history.

In contrast to these successful efforts at decapitation, the U.S. attempt in 1961 to overthrow Fidel Castro as prime minister of Cuba failed utterly. A brigade of 1,400 CIA-trained Cuban exiles landed at the Bay of Pigs intending to attract enough popular support to mount a revolution that would eventually unseat Castro. On paper, he had some 30,000 regular troops under his command, and he could call upon a further 200,000 militiamen, though it was unclear how politically reliable they would prove to be. As events were to show, the CIA had greatly underestimated how loyal Castro's forces would be to him. Some of the brigade's landing craft foundered in the bay, and those exiles who made it ashore never received the anticipated support of the local Cuban population. The White House, which continued to deny American involvement throughout the operation (and beyond), eventually decided to cut its losses and refused to commit additional military resources to the invasion. As a result, the brigade failed to secure a foothold on the island, and most of its troops either surrendered or became casualties. Some of the prisoners were executed, though Castro later agreed to return the others in exchange for cash, food, and medical supplies. Over the ensuing years, the United States made several other attempts to remove the Cuban dictator from power, but none succeeded.

Decapitation and targeted killing are increasingly attractive to Western policymakers largely because of the increased reach and greater accuracy of modern airpower. Weaponized drones and stealth aircraft especially, seem to offer the possibility of conducting precise attacks against hostile leaders, thereby affecting radical political change from afar but with much lower risk than typically is involved with using ground forces. As an example, military advisors and defense pundits enthusiastically discussed the possibility of decapitating Saddam Hussein's regime through airpower alone before the First Gulf War (1990–91). As General Michael Dugan of the U.S. Air Force argued, Saddam Hussein was a "one-man show" in Iraq and without him, Iraqi troops would quickly "lose their legitimacy and ... be back in Iraq in a matter of hours."

By destroying targets in Iraq, Dugan added, the U.S.-led coalition would "convince [the Iraqi] population that [Saddam Hussein] and his regime cannot protect them," thereby undermining his leadership and authority. However, the White House rejected the idea on the grounds that it meant expanding the war beyond the coalition's objectives (i.e., the liberation of Kuwait), and Dugan was summarily relieved of his post. Nor was it clear who or what would have filled the resultant power vacuum in Iraq or how— with a crippled communications infrastructure—that person or group could have ordered the Iraqi army's withdrawal from Kuwait, if in fact that army did not disintegrate as Dugan predicted. Although his ideas were dismissed, they were not unusual for airpower theorists at the time.

One such theorist was Colonel John Warden of the U.S. Air Force, whose concepts relate directly to decapitation and targeted killing.

Warden believed that precision airstrikes could sap a foe's willingness to fight without causing undue casualties and collateral damage. Warden's theory likened an opponent to a dynamic system of five interconnected subsystems: leadership, organic or system essentials (raw materials, energy and food sources, etc.), communications and transportation infrastructures, population, and fielded military forces. He depicted these graphically as a series of concentric circles or "rings," which earned Warden the moniker "Lord of the Rings." The object of any modern air campaign would then be to identify the critical points in each ring and to attack them systematically until the opponent either surrendered or became paralyzed strategically. Attacking critical points in the leadership ring in particular, would separate the "head of the snake" from its body, thus effecting decapitation, and deprive hostile forces of their guiding intelligence. Warden's theory is problematic in the sense that strategic paralysis, if it were to occur, could well prevent an opponent from complying with one's will. However, the theory also had obvious applications as a form of targeted killing, since the specific points to be attacked could be adjusted as desired, either as a prelude to, or in lieu of, full decapitation.

Warden's five rings model

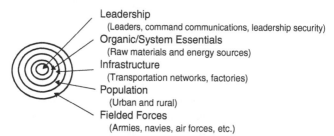

Leadership
(Leaders, command communications, leadership security)
Organic/System Essentials
(Raw materials and energy sources)
Infrastructure
(Transportation networks, factories)
Population
(Urban and rural)
Fielded Forces
(Armies, navies, air forces, etc.)

7. **Warden's five rings portray an opponent as an integrated system consisting of key leaders and their chief means of communication and control, energy production facilities, transportation infrastructure, population, and deployed military forces. By launching precise attacks against specific points in this system, Warden believed, one could cause it to collapse.**

The United States and its coalition partners finally succeeded in removing Saddam Hussein from power in a decapitation operation in 2003. Before the main military offensive, CIA operatives worked at driving a wedge between the Iraqi military and its head of state. For the most part this effort succeeded, and large numbers of Iraqi regular units surrendered, though some Republican Guard and irregular forces remained loyal to him. Iraq was subsequently overrun by Coalition forces and Saddam Hussein was captured; however, the coalition found itself unprepared to confront a budding civil war between religious and political factions vying for influence and control over Iraq's future. In short, although the decapitation phase of the operation was accomplished successfully, the coalition struggled with assisting the Iraqis to establish a viable and representative successor regime.

As Clausewitz once noted, an insurrection's center of gravity—the person, thing, or idea that is vital to holding an organization or movement together—consists of its principal leaders and public opinion. One way to think about decapitation, then, is to view it as an attack against *half* an insurgency's center of gravity. Without appropriate measures for addressing the other half, the task of putting down an insurgency is likely to grow more difficult over time.

Targeted killing

If decapitation is an attack on half an insurrection's center of gravity, then one way to view targeted killing is as the systematic decimation of the insurgency's rank and file. As a form of selective attrition, its application must be controlled and weighed against the potential for causing collateral damage or a moral backlash. Under President Obama, the American use of targeted killings in Iraq and Afghanistan expanded greatly with the employment of drones. They have targeted not only key leaders, but also many

8. A U.S. Predator drone flying over a desert landscape in southern California in 2012. Armed drones have become a common, but highly controversial, weapon for conducting assassinations of terrorists and criminals.

mid-level managers, and in some cases even lower ranking fighters. By 2012, some reports claimed that between 1,500 and 2,600 militants had been killed by drone strikes; by 2014, and after greater scrutiny, the total was reckoned to be closer to 2,400. Priority generally went to eliminating those who coordinated militant strikes, experts who constructed improvised explosive devices (IEDs), those personnel who provided or arranged for logistical support, and groups of individual fighters.

Such an offensive might dissuade some would-be insurgents from joining an organization that is under attack and might convince some of those who are already members to desert their groups. As one former Taliban leader admitted, "American operations are very effective; the night raids, the airstrikes and ground attacks...I was afraid they would kill me too." Obviously, such confessions can result from a captive's tendency to tell interviewers what they want to hear. We must also weigh such statements against whether violent militant acts actually rose or declined during the period, and why. Contrary to expectations, for instance, reports published around 2013 by the defense consulting firm RAND and by the U.S. State Department showed a rise in terrorism globally, despite a concerted targeted-killing campaign. Targeted killings might not contribute directly to an increase or a decrease in terrorist or insurgent incidents. Other factors usually are involved, such as renewed sectarian fighting, support from neighboring states that allowed militant groups to retreat to safe havens and rearm and refit, and the political or seasonal timing of insurgent counteroffensives. Targeted killing may accomplish little more than "mowing the grass" in some situations. Still, that may be all one wishes or is able to do.

Targeted killing can prove useful in situations in which decapitation will not work or when an organization's complete collapse is not desired. Decapitation works best against a centralized foe. However, many contemporary terrorist and insurgent groups are decentralized, that is, they have no single head. Rather, each "snake" has many heads. Moreover, some groups have found ways to adapt to decapitation of their leaders by preparing mid-level leaders to step in swiftly when the principals are killed or captured. Several Hamas leaders have been eliminated over the years by Israeli attacks, for instance; but in each case the organization's effectiveness was impaired only briefly, until second-tier leaders ascended to fill the gaps. Similarly, officials once believed al-Qaeda in Iraq had been all but vanquished; but, instead, some of its followers migrated to other organizations, especially, the one known as Daesh, or the "Islamic State of Iraq and Syria" (ISIS), the "Islamic State of Iraq and the Levant" (ISIL), or simply the "Islamic State." In such cases, targeted killing can enable states to keep pressure on such organizations and to restrict their movements while other strategies or policies are developed.

Neither decapitation nor targeted killing will necessarily destroy an organization permanently. Nonetheless, both can degrade its effectiveness for a time. Most research, in fact, shows that any leadership turnover, violent or otherwise, contributes to a degradation in organizational performance. Sustained leadership turnover appears to contribute to a group's demise over the long term. This is true whether the organizations are regular military units or irregular gangs. Casualties are expected in war, and for that reason most organizations have some resilience built into them, or they develop it if given enough time. Hence decapitation and targeted killing should be seen not only as temporary solutions, but also as temporal ones, with windows of opportunity meant to be exploited quickly. When that does not occur, the result is usually a strategy of attrition competing against a strategy of exhaustion in a race against time.

As Machiavelli keenly observed, killing the leader and his closest cohorts will seldom suffice for lasting success. The survivors are likely to have an interest in overthrowing any foreign regime. His opinion was borne out in a sense in 2003 when the U.S.-led coalition disbanded the Ba'ath party and, with it, Iraq's centralized structure of authority. At the same time, it is easy to take Machiavelli's statement out of context. He was referring not only to conquest by decapitation, but also to holding on to and managing one's conquests thereafter. His statement thus pertains to managing the aftermath of regime change. This is the chief problem with a political goal such as regime change, and one that policymakers and military strategists must consider beforehand. As the legacy of Chile's General Pinochet shows, regime change does not always result in a better peace.

From the standpoint of collapsing an organization, decapitation runs the obvious risk of removing from power the person or group who actually can order opposing military forces to stop fighting. To illustrate the problem with an analogy, if the adversary were an octopus rather than a snake, the head might indeed be severed from the body, yet the individual legs and tentacles can still inflict a great deal of harm. Even if only one of the tentacles manages to detonate a weapon of mass destruction, that lone incident could cause enough physical and psychological damage to force an administration to step down. Under such circumstances, pursuing a strategy of decapitation would be counterproductive.

To reduce the effectiveness of targeted killing and to make it more difficult to execute politically, militant groups may try to move into densely populated areas so they can use noncombatants as human shields. Such countermeasures will put more pressure on ensuring the accuracy of one's intelligence, and they will likely restrict the frequency and timing of targeted strikes. Even if little or no collateral damage occurs, hostile groups may launch sophisticated information campaigns claiming it has done so. For that and other reasons, such operations require highly trained personnel and state-of-the-art equipment, since conscripts, however willing, are less likely to possess the requisite skills.

Success with targeted killing depends on many of the same factors as a strategy of attrition. Quantitative analysis might not capture progress (or its opposite) accurately. As with any strategy, reliable intelligence concerning a group's basic strengths and weaknesses and its lines of succession is essential. It also is useful to employ multiple or nested strategies whenever possible, so that one's opponent has more than one problem to confront. For instance, one might consider employing decapitation in conjunction with diplomatic and information campaigns aimed at causing divisions among the opposing groups. These strategies could be paired, in turn, with attrition strategies that sever or disrupt the group's lifelines. Some groups can be bribed into cooperating; some can be co-opted in other ways.

In sum, the utility of decapitation or targeted killing, as with any strategy, depends on the conditions under which they are used, and on what one wishes to achieve. It is not always desirable, nor even possible, to address the root causes of a conflict. This is particularly true if one lacks the will or wherewithal to arrive at a durable solution, which is often the case.

In such situations, temporary disruption of a militant group's operations or reduction of its overall effectiveness may be all that is possible or desired. Decapitation and targeted killing can also serve the purposes of policy by sending "messages" not only to opponents, but also to domestic audiences. They also can satisfy public cries for retaliation (which admittedly may only add to the cycle of violence). Given reliable intelligence, either strategy can help preempt attacks or delay undesirable events, such as the development of nuclear programs by rival powers. Decapitation and targeted killing also can buy time for one's strategic situation to change, so as to allow the entry of new allies or partners who may perhaps be better equipped to resolve a difficult situation. A very real risk exists, however, that choosing to buy time—and thus avoiding the problem instead of solving it—can become an egregiously difficult habit to overcome.

Chapter 7
Winning without fighting: information and cyber power

Sun Tzu once wrote that the most skillful military strategists are those able to win without fighting: "Those skilled in war subdue the enemy's army without battle. They capture his cities without assaulting them and overthrow his state without protracted operations." History has largely obscured what Sun Tzu really meant, but the idea of winning without fighting is one that would appeal to any era because of its lower risks and costs. However, bloodless victories are rare for good reasons; they can require special capabilities and skills, among which are the clever use of information and deception.

Cyber power has brought capabilities related to information manipulation (which, henceforth in this discussion includes misinformation and disinformation) and deception to bear in the twenty-first century. Even if it might not eliminate the need for fighting altogether, cyber power offers opportunities to weaken our foe's material capacity and willingness to fight in ways that approximate Sun Tsu's ideal. Cyber power cannot physically subdue militaries. But it can aid in disrupting their command and control and their lines of communication and supply. Cyber power cannot capture cities. But it can assist in making life in them difficult by shutting down critical infrastructure—the electrical grids, gas lines, transportation hubs, and so on—that enables energy, food, and health supplies to flow into urban areas and allows them to function. Cyber power cannot overthrow a state. But it can influence a state's citizenry with information that weakens trust in the government, its political systems, its social institutions, and goes further to exacerbate tensions and divisions among its populations. Why risk overthrowing a state if it is less costly to render it a weak and dependent puppet instead?

To be sure, substantial controversy has surrounded the efficacy of cyber power. Pundits have long warned of the possibility of "Cyber-Armageddons" or "Cyber-Pearl Harbors," that could render states defenseless. But these warnings were alarmist, for such attacks have not occurred. Moreover, despite the hyperbole, the effects of cyberattacks have thus far been short-lived. They generate annoying interruptions in services and communications, but states and organizations prepared for such attacks can carry out repairs in a matter of hours or days, making the damage disruptive but temporary. Ukraine suffered through severe Russian cyberattacks from 2013 through 2015, but it learned from them. As a result, it was able to respond more appropriately when Russian cyberattacks came again in 2022. Furthermore, few deaths have been directly associated with cyberattacks, though cybercrime, such as identity theft, and cyber-espionage can cause great harm to individuals as well as to major organizations. For many strategic analysts, therefore, cyber power remains more rhetorical than real.

Despite the underwhelming results delivered by cyber power, practically every modern state has established military or private cybersecurity organizations to create or to enhance their defenses against cyberattacks. Cyber Command in the United States and Cyber Force in the United Kingdom are but two examples. The establishment of these and similar organizations indicates how seriously cyber threats are being taken by those in positions of responsibility. Cyber power itself has become an essential instrument of national policy, much like other forms of national power. In truth, even naysayers agree its use in conjunction with other forms of national power can prove synergistic. Cyber competition among states, semi-state actors (independent organizations employed by states), and nonstate actors, moreover, is fierce and ongoing with no end in sight.

Cyber power

Simply put, cyber power is the ability to operate with *relative* security and freedom of action within cyberspace. Most experts believe achieving absolute security and freedom of action within cyberspace is impossible. But that is true for any type of domain whether land, sea, air, or outer space. The fact that cyber power can be used for nefarious purposes is the other side of the proverbial coin. Power itself is neutral. The purposes to which it is put determine whether it is being used for good or ill.

Unfortunately, cyber power has been conflated with the more provocative term "cyber war" or "cyber warfare," which has inspired the ire of critics. While it is true "cyber battles" occur almost continuously among contending groups (states, semi-state actors, and violent nonstate actors), confusing cyber warfare with cyber power is unhelpful. For purposes of clarity, we can think of cyber warfare as the use of digital code to inflict physical or psychological harm on other parties to coerce or co-opt them.

Cyber warfare

Cyber warfare involves a three-way competition over the rapid migration of essential data and functions to online networks, which creates lucrative targets; the efforts of cybersecurity systems, which struggle to protect those networks; and the attempts of cyber-attackers, whether state-sponsored

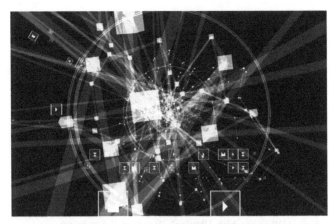

9. This illustration of war in cyberspace is one of a series developed by Project X of the U.S. Defense Advanced Research Projects Agency (DARPA) to help cyber warriors envision warfare in the digital universe and to enable them to design better cyber operations.

organizations or independent or semi-independent criminals, who find ways to defeat those security measures.

Some cyberattacks aim at inflicting financial damage on individuals, such as through targeted sanctions that freeze bank accounts and block transactions. These measures can support a government's policy of punishing criminal behavior; they can also be used by criminal hackers as a form of blackmail. But states have attempted to employ other types of cyberattacks to achieve strategic effects through the manipulation of information on a larger scale, which in turn can facilitate the manipulation of target populations. The goals of this type of "social manipulation" include interference in political elections, the shaping of public opinion, and consumer preferences and habits, as well as social norms, group identities, and cultural values. Some salient examples include Russian attempts to influence the U.S. elections in 2016 and 2020, in addition to the Kremlin's creation of "deep

Anonymous ✔
@YourAnonOne · Follow

The #Anonymous collective is officially in cyber war against the pro-Russian hacker group #Killnet.

12:20 PM · May 21, 2022   ⓘ

💜 **43.8K**   💬 **Reply**   ⬆ **Share**

---

10. Cyber power has made it both possible and popular for various groups to participate in war, either for their own ends or in support of the belligerents.

fakes" in 2023 in which Ukraine's President Zelensky was depicted as requesting surrender terms.

Cyberattacks can also facilitate the dissemination of propaganda and the waging of information warfare. But this strand of cyberwarfare has evolved beyond a mere competition in strategic communications into a hacktivists' free-for-all. Hacktivists, such as the pro-Russian group Killnet, claimed to have conducted attacks that have disrupted Ukrainian supply chains and logistics, thereby driving up the costs of financing the war by hundreds of millions of dollars. Pro-Ukrainian hacktivists, such as the IT Army of Ukraine, made similar claims. Common cyberattacks by these groups included denial-of-service attacks against infrastructure, gas and oil companies, and respective stock exchanges. The result was an explosion of independent and semi-independent or state-sponsored hacktivism in which engaged parties may support one side or the other as a means of pursuing larger political agendas.

Cyber strategy

Cyber strategies must accommodate cyber power's special attributes. These fall into two categories: physical and functional.

Their physical attributes include terminals, nodes, and conduits, which provide network connectivity. With connectivity, we can launch cyberattacks from anywhere on the globe, even from within the target country. We can also use a single code to attack multiple targets, at designated times, for specific periods, and without creating logistical demands or necessarily revealing one's identity. Unlike most types of military power, cyber power has the advantage of not needing to cause human casualties, which makes it a political asset rather than a liability. It can, however, produce extensive collateral damage by unintentionally infecting nontargeted systems. Naturally, a steady power supply is also vital for connectivity and therefore represents a critical vulnerability for cyber power. Simply put, without connectivity, there is no cyber power.

Cyber power's functional attributes consist of its capacity to gain access to, to manipulate, and to represent data. The factors of time, distance, terrain, and weather are not relevant to cyber power from a functional standpoint. Compared with economic power, for instance, which, though potent, can take months, even years, to achieve the desired effects, cyber power can achieve immediate effects, or have its effects released over a prolonged period. Terrain and weather, however, can affect cyber power's physical attributes.

Cyber power's functional attributes enable a host of common cyber tactics to include "honey-pot traps" that lure users to counterfeit sites and then gather information about the users themselves; "digital decoys" can be loaded with falsified data to confuse or sabotage would-be attackers; remotely controlled "botnets" (robot networks) which can trick or deceive hostile users; methods of IP-address and signature identification that can enable the identification and tracking of an attacker; and backdoor infiltration techniques, such as Trojan horses, phishing schemes, and spearing attacks, which can trick rival systems into allowing access; and the transmission of infected links or emails that can sabotage or stymie adversary systems.

Cyber tactics can be combined into cyber operations, which in turn can be combined into cyber campaigns, which can contribute to the realization of cyber strategies. Indeed, some cyber actors—states, semi-state organizations, or nonstate groups—now think more routinely about achieving strategic effects through cyber power. More precisely, they see cyber power as a way to advance strategic, even grand strategic, goals. One such goal might be to tip the regional balance of power in one's favor gradually. Cyber operations might thus be aimed at stealing information related to various weapon systems or defensive plans, or to obtain control or influence over portions of vital supply chains. Individually, such operations might appear to other states as episodic breaches of security, or periodic upticks in economic competition. They will also have the advantage of staying under the threshold of armed conflict, even though their collective results might at one point place the perpetrating state in a dominant bargaining or hegemonic position.

Like other types of strategy, cyber strategies can be of an offensive or defensive nature. Originally, cyber power was thought to be strongest when used offensively. That belief was overturned in 2022 and 2023 when the Ukrainians, with Western help and having already experienced Russian cyberattacks, used cyber power effectively in a defensive role. Nonetheless, we would do well to avoid rigid rules about whether the offense or defense is stronger in cyberwarfare. Technological innovations occur too quickly within the cyber domain for us to entertain such rules.

Attribution, knowing who was responsible for an attack (or defense), was once considered impossible to determine in cyberspace. According to political science theory, without attribution, cyber actors would not be able to derive genuine political value from their actions, thereby undermining their ability to compel or deter a rival. That, in turn, could eliminate the rationale for conducting them in the first place. But cyber forensics, especially when corroborated through other sources of intelligence, have developed to the point that attribution no longer poses an insurmountable problem. Rather, the problem is how to conceal one's identity.

Nor is attribution always necessary to achieve one's objectives. Heads of state from Mao Zedong to Vladimir Putin have taken credit, or been assigned blame, for many abuses of power. They have benefited politically in many cases, despite what the facts might have said. Indeed, political value, however vague or temporary, accrues in multiple ways and can be appropriated by determined political actors. Mao did that during the Chinese Civil War, when he and his Communist Party took credit for any successful counterattack against the Japanese invader, while at the same time criticizing Chiang Kai-shek's Nationalist Party for idleness and incompetence. Political value can also accrue even when one denies responsibility for an action. This was known as "plausible deniability" during the Cold War, and it meant an actor could deny an action, even though no one was fooled by the denial. Contrary to political science theory, in other words, the difficulty of achieving verifiable attribution may make cyber power more useful as a clandestine or covert political instrument.

Cyber operations

Cyber operations conducted in support of a military strategy can take multiple forms. But it can be useful to group them under three categories: those aimed at *denying* access to data, those designed to *intervene* and collect data, and those intended to *manipulate* data.

Denial operations block access to critical information or activities, such as financial transactions, energy production and transfer, intelligence gathering, or routine communications. They typically involve "distributed denial of service" attacks (DDoS). But they also can include a combination of policy- and cyber-blacklisting. Examples of these are the U.S. Treasury Department's fiscal isolation of known members of al-Qaeda, ISIS; certain officials in Iran, Iraq, North Korea, and Syria; as well as numerous Russian oligarchs. Banks and financial institutions are advised against conducting transactions with blacklisted individuals or organizations. Ignoring the advisories will result in the banks and institutions being designated "enablers or associates of terrorism," at which point their IP addresses will be denied access to U.S. financial systems. This type of denial operation restricts one's the ability to raise capital and move it around in support of an operation.

Targeted sanctions, such as banning travel and freezing financial assets, against foreign elites or individual companies, are another form of denial. The effectiveness of sanctions is a matter of debate due to the availability of workarounds. Adversaries expect to be targeted and make their plans accordingly. But that is not a reflection on the limits of cyber power as much as it is on the range of sanctions being imposed. Ultimately, sanctions may not be enough to compel or deter potential belligerents.

Of course, denial operations cannot shutdown all means of internet communication for criminals or terrorists. Nonetheless, better investigative and forensic techniques have increased the risks of using cyber power. Although cyberspace and social media have enhanced the ability of criminals and terrorists to recruit, for instance, these means have also strengthened the ability of heads of state to detect and to hinder or block such activity.

Intervention operations aim to penetrate cyber defenses to reach data servers and to eavesdrop and collect intelligence, also known as cyber espionage. Cyber espionage is the illicit appropriation of sensitive information by accessing other computer systems or networks. Examples of cyber espionage include the 2015 attack on the U.S. Office of Personnel Management, as well as the 2003 "Titan Rain" attacks, which targeted the U.S. Departments of Defense, State, and Homeland Security over several years. These attacks, which were traced to a cyber-organization within China, were evidently intended to steal the identities of as many U.S. government employees as possible and then to use those identities to gain greater access to other sensitive networks.

Manipulation operations can be extensive. They endeavor to sabotage or disrupt systems to "crash" them, or to make them yield outcomes different from those intended. A common way of accomplishing cyber manipulation is through a malicious code or virus (malware) that spreads to other systems. Disruption entails undermining the control or authority of a system.

Manipulating an adversary's systems can be more advantageous than destroying them. But it requires attackers to remain undetected for a certain length of time. The so-called Stuxnet virus, which disabled computer systems in Iran's Natanz nuclear plant, a form of cyber sabotage, is an example of this type of manipulation.

Manipulation also can facilitate economic or financial warfare. Economic warfare is essentially a competition for the control of goods and services. Financial warfare is the competition for the control of the credit and monetary foundations that underpin an economy, particularly regarding production and distribution. Financial warfare aims to disrupt an adversary's ability to conduct essential monetary activities, such as pricing goods, setting exchange rates, and forming capital. It also includes "currency wars," the devaluation of an adversary's currency via market manipulation. Cyber power can facilitate both economic and financial warfare because of connectivity. As the West's economic and financial warfare against Russia for its invasion of Ukraine show, however, the effects of such operations can require considerable time to be realized.

Cyber power and social manipulation

Cyber power has also created opportunities for another, broader form of manipulation—social manipulation. This form of manipulation consists of targeting social groups with a blend of information, misinformation, and disinformation to achieve a variety of effects, which might include reducing a group's capacity or willingness to fight, to shape a group's perceptions in ways that exacerbate tension and discord, or which enable populations to be managed better by their governments. Social manipulation uses many of the techniques of traditional forms of psychological warfare, information warfare, and cognitive warfare. However, it also benefits from the greater reach and speed of contemporary cyber power coupled with the enhanced access provided by popular social media platforms such as Facebook, Google+, Instagram, Snapchat, TikTok, Twitter, WhatsApp, and YouTube.

The art of social manipulation itself is as old as antiquity. Marketing strategies, for instance, have long manipulated human perceptions through slogans and schemes to increase sales and raise profit margins. An example is the tactic automobile retailers employ when they first show customers the manufacturer's suggested retail price (MSRP) for a vehicle, then list several rebates and discounts, all of which result in a lower price. Customers will typically anchor on the first figure they are shown (the "anchoring effect" in human biases) which, as retailers hope, is more likely to make the final price seem like a bargain to the consumer, even if the price for the vehicle is still high. This is an example of benign social manipulation. Other uses are indeed possible. Research into cognitive biases by two Israeli psychologists, Amos Tversky and Daniel Kahneman, in 1974, for instance, has changed the way we think about human decision-making and is moving social manipulation from an art to a science. More work remains to be done in this field, however, as enthusiastic researchers have discovered more than 200 biases, a number that likely needs to be culled. Also, behavioral scientists, not wanting to be left out, have added several more to the list.

Research by scholars from Oxford's Internet Institute (OII) reveals numerous efforts to use social media platforms to shape public opinion, influence a government's policy choices, voter turnout during elections, and to spread fear and distrust in some cases. OII research shows more than 80 countries have established special (official and unofficial) "cyber troops" expressly for these purposes. Terms such as industrialized disinformation, information manipulation, social media manipulation, and computational propaganda describe various aspects of their efforts. Of these terms, only computational propaganda is not self-explanatory: it is information or misinformation, such as "junk news" or "fake news" or "manipulation narratives," transmitted by bots or trolls or similar means through social media to mislead or confuse target populations. Sometimes the most effective approach is not to change perceptions or behavior, which can be exceedingly difficult, but rather to reinforce them: to make target populations more extreme in their views by convincing them to remain impervious to other perspectives. Such objectives promote political disputes and social discord already in play.

Perhaps the most salient example of an attempt at social manipulation occurred during the 2016 U.S. presidential election when an organization called the Internet Research Agency (IRA), a Russian troll farm, endeavored to influence the outcome of the election. The IRA gained access to multiple social media platforms including Facebook, Google+, PayPal, Tumbler, and YouTube, and used various forms of misinformation to dissuade minorities from voting and to encourage conservative voters to take to the polls in greater numbers. The IRA reached an estimated 126 million people on Facebook alone. In the end, the

Republicans won the election, which satisfied the IRA's goal. However, it was not clear whether the outcome was due primarily (or at all) to the IRA's efforts, since the Democratic candidate won the popular vote by a margin of several million. Nonetheless, the IRA did exacerbate divisions within American society and raise concerns about the integrity of the U.S. electoral process. An investigation by the Senate Select Intelligence Committee, published in 2020, in fact found evidence of Russian interference, but it also concluded the interference had not altered the election results. More safeguards were subsequently put in place to protect the U.S. election system prior to the presidential election of 2020.

Russian efforts at social manipulation are believed to have derived from the concept of "reflexive control," a form of perception management. Reflexive control means using deception (*maskirovka*) to shape environments in ways that trick foes into making decisions a rival wants them to make, or ones that weaken their position without them necessarily realizing it. The theory was developed in the 1960s by a Russian psychologist and mathematician named Vladimir Lefebvre. Reflexive control requires knowing one's adversaries well enough to know what their choices will be beforehand. Only in that way can information, misinformation, and disinformation be used appropriately.

By all accounts, Russian efforts at reflexive control are more effective at manipulating their domestic populations than foreign ones. Assessments of Russian information warfare in the conflict against Ukraine, for instance, have revealed them to be too clumsy and crude to be credible. By contrast, many accounts claim the Peoples Republic of China has become a "surveillance state," in which artificial intelligence and cyber-based observation technologies are combined to manipulate, if not control, its populations. The actual amount of control the Chinese government enjoys over its populations may be much less than it desires. But the influence it has over social media, its proliferation of facial recognition and tracking technologies, and the narratives it employs through all media outlets make its posture of social control credible.

While social manipulation is rapidly evolving from an art into a science, so too are the safeguards against interference and manipulation. Artificial intelligence is at work on both sides of the problem. Perhaps one indispensable safeguard is for populations to take the information they receive from social media platforms and other sources with a healthy dose of skepticism. But that may be easier said than done as artificial intelligence continues to render everything, and its opposite, more authentic.

In any case, the possibility of winning without fighting is no longer a lofty ideal. It can be done in small ways or in grandiose ones. But it is likely to be most effective when the subterfuges are subtle enough to avoid detection, and when the objectives are limited, or located just below the threshold of armed conflict, in the so-called gray zone.

Chapter 8
What causes military strategies to succeed or fail?

Most experts would agree the practice of military strategy is fraught generally with misjudgments, miscalculations, and missteps on all sides. Strategy is easy to understand but difficult to execute. Even when military commanders possess exceptional skills, they frequently lack the full authority to attack who, what, when, where, and how they wish; nor do they necessarily have enough of the right means at hand to execute the ideal strategy. Instead, what typically happens is the opposing sides do their best to pursue victory in an environment characterized by chance and uncertainty. André Beaufre, a twentieth-century French general and military theorist, fittingly referred to this clash of opposing expectations of victory as strategy's dialectic. The back-and-forth nature of this dialectic, in which strategies might be thoroughly altered, can make for some very untidy consequences, and all but ensure ideal outcomes rarely, if ever, occur.

Given the many constraints of the real world, how then should military strategists improve their odds of success while reducing their chances of failure?

What enables military strategies to succeed?

Numerous theories explain why strategies succeed or fail. Ultimately, though, a successful military strategy is simply one that works. Nothing in war is certain, but nothing in war should be left to chance either. Taking all the right steps will not guarantee victory, but doing so can tip the odds in one's favor.

Among the myriad tasks that need to happen for a strategy to succeed, four stand out, though the sequence in which they should occur is by no means rigid, and some can occur concurrently. The first task is conducting a critical appraisal of the adversary's strengths and weaknesses and matching those against one's own. The result should be a totally objective overall assessment that must be updated as new information becomes available, and as the war's circumstances change. As Sun Tzu advised, "Know the enemy and know yourself, and in a hundred battles you will never be in peril. If you are ignorant of the enemy but know yourself," he added, "your chances of winning and losing are equal; if ignorant both of your enemy and of yourself, you are certain in every battle to be in peril."

Second, this net assessment should serve as a baseline for developing courses of action that weaken the foe enough to get what one wants. One of the oldest recorded instances of such an assessment was composed in 1194 by the medieval churchman and writer Gerald of Wales; it described the strengths and weaknesses of the Welsh, from the tactical advantages afforded by their countryside to the temperament and character of their clans to the particular cultural practices that rendered them vulnerable to a strategy based on economic warfare, concentric military pressure, and "dividing and conquering." In the war of 1276–77, King Edward I of England purportedly succeeded in conquering Wales by following a plan similar to that outlined by Gerald.

Third, the head of state must select a military commander with the knowledge and level of competence needed to develop and implement the desired strategy. Finding the right commander can take time. U.S. President Abraham Lincoln fired six generals before he found one, in Ulysses S. Grant, capable of defeating the Confederacy's armies consistently enough to bring the war to an end. British prime minister Winston Churchill went through three generals before he found one, in Bernard L. Montgomery, capable of defeating Erwin Rommel, the Wehrmacht's famed "Desert Fox." As historians have noted, the strategist is probably more important than the strategy because one needs wisdom to know when and how to adjust one's strategy, and this quality is critical for success. In short, the execution of any strategy will likely fail unless the hand of the strategist directing it is a skilled one.

For this reason, accurate knowledge of an opposing strategist is pertinent to one's assessment. As the Greek historian Polybius wrote, "There is no more precious asset for a general than knowledge of his opponent's guiding principles and character, and anyone who thinks the opposite is at once blind and foolish." Polybius had in mind the example of Hannibal, who exploited key personality traits of several of Rome's commanders to defeat them.

The Greek historian's advice holds even for the conditions of modern warfare. As in cards, playing one's opponent is just as important as playing one's hand. The generals of antiquity acquired information about their opponents largely through spies and by interrogating captives and local inhabitants. Today, knowledge of enemy leaders is obtained not only through spies, but also through more highly technical means of intelligence collection and dissemination, including electronic eavesdropping, satellite imagery, and cyber espionage.

Although intelligence is often incomplete and is sometimes distorted by institutional pressures, it is essential to discover as much as possible about one's foes (and friends), whether they are heads of state or tribal chieftains. Not only is knowledge of an opposing commander important, so too is intelligence regarding the type of force under that person's direction—its morale or fighting spirit, the quality and quantity of its weaponry, and its basic tactics and ways of fighting.

Fourth, coherent and comprehensive war plans are needed to pull everything together. The war plan is the practical face of strategy and is the real link between policy aims and the use of military force to achieve those aims. It is here that the components of strategy come into play. The war plan establishes military objectives, sets the parameters for campaigns, and assigns tasks and subtasks to specific commanders, who then can be held accountable for achieving them, and it identifies details that must be dealt with lest they hinder the plan's execution. The war plan, or a plan of campaign, can be direct and brutal in character, as was the case with U.S. General William T. Sherman's march on Atlanta in December 1864; or it can be indirect yet simple, as was General Erich von Manstein's plan for Hitler's conquest of France in 1940.

Each of these examples also illustrates a fundamental difference in orientation: Sherman's campaign was oriented on terrain, Manstein's on enemy forces. The former can be said to be Jominian in character in that it seeks to control (or neutralize) the "decisive points of a theater of war," such as cities, depots, fortresses, and transportation hubs. The force-oriented approach can be likened to that of Clausewitz, who advised studying battles and engagements, what goes into winning them, and how to use the outcomes of such encounters for the purpose of the war. Neither orientation wholly excludes the other.

It should be clear by now military strategy is much more than pushing steel across a battle area—whether it be land, sea, or aerospace—to destroy enemy forces. It requires a deft hand capable of balancing not just ends, ways, means, and risk, but also two potentially divergent tasks: that of weakening an adversary's capacity to fight and that of achieving the war's purpose.

Often, these tasks draw one's efforts in opposite directions—with military commanders pursuing the first and political leaders looking to accomplish the second and to keep costs down. Military strategists must ensure that the foe's resistance is sufficiently broken; otherwise, the war may drag on. Yet they must do so in ways that accommodate the broader agendas of policymakers, which, in turn, often desire maximum flexibility, especially as the course of events gives rise to unanticipated opportunities. It is not always wise to abandon one's original goals to pursue such opportunities, tempting as they may be. History is replete with examples of heads of state and generals, who, whether influenced by hubris or greed, imprudently attempted to seize goals beyond the reach of their military power. Napoleon and Hitler, for instance, were both guilty of what some might call "imperial overstretch," particularly as regards their fateful decisions to invade Russia. On the other hand, the failure to exploit opportunities can lead to greater costs, perhaps prolonging the conflict or causing it to fail.

What causes military strategies to fail?

Obviously, military strategies fail when they lack some of the elements crucial to success, namely, objective assessments, sound courses of action, expert military commanders, and war plans coherent enough to pull everything together. During the Second World War, Germany and Japan each had capable commanders and disciplined military forces; however, their hubris, combined with the racial biases and antipathies inherent in their ideologies, made it difficult to produce objective assessments. Consequently, their military strategies and plans were based on faulty assumptions and cognitive biases regarding the reach of their own armed forces and what they could conquer and hold, as well as their underestimation of the willingness of the Soviet Union and the Western democracies to continue fighting in the face of heavy casualties.

Some critics attribute strategic failure to the inherent difficulty of implementing any strategy or war plan. Factors such as incidental friction, weather, misinformation, misunderstandings, bureaucratic inertia, defection, treason, and similar misfortunes certainly can cause operations to fail and otherwise sensible plans to collapse. As Clausewitz observed, "In war, everything is simple, but even the simplest thing is difficult." These factors, however, affect both sides, and any responsible military planner will take them into account. They may make success difficult, but they do not guarantee failure.

Instead, a larger factor has more bearing on the question of winning or losing. Experts will offer elaborate theories and lengthy lists explaining why failure occurred. But the most important reason a military strategy fails is because the opposing party refused to concede, even when its continued resistance was patently self-destructive. Continuing to resist can drive up the costs of a conflict until they exceed its anticipated benefits, causing political division and disillusionment, and perhaps ultimately wearing down an adversary's resolve. The key variable in success, therefore, is the opposing party's willingness to resist, how strong it is and why. The rub is whether breaking that will or co-opting it can be accomplished with available resources and courses of action and without jeopardizing one's long-term interests. Sometimes it cannot be done.

Resembling the process of bartering, many strategic dialectics end without a clear winner or loser, but with each party getting enough to justify its sacrifices and to claim victory. Some military strategies, such as deterrence, may continue indefinitely, in "quasi-win-win" situations, where the aim is to dissuade attack. Others, such as decapitation, ultimately may benefit both parties by leading to better relations, regardless of the original cause of

117

hostilities. Still others, such as targeted killing, may persist because neither party possesses the wherewithal or the willingness to do more; one party may simply find it politically beneficial to have a manageable threat at hand rather than to eliminate it altogether. Therefore, the general assumption that half of all strategies must fail (since only one side can win) is simply not always true. Neither war nor strategy is necessarily a zero-sum game. Many armed conflicts end in negotiated settlements, and, in the grand scheme of things, these arrangements might produce only a temporary peace.

References

Prologue

The purported conversation between the American and Vietnamese
colonels is recounted in Harry G. Summers Jr., *On Strategy: A
Critical Analysis of the Vietnam War* (Novato, CA: Presidio, 1995),
preface.

Chapter 1: What is military strategy?

Clausewitz's definition of strategy may be found in Carl von
Clausewitz, *On War*, translated by Michael and Peter Paret
(Princeton, NJ: Princeton University Press, 1986), 177.
Jomini's definition of strategy can be found in Antoine Henri Jomini,
The Art of War, translated by G. H. Mendell and W. P. Craighill
(1862; repr., Westport, CT: Greenwood, 1971), 62.
Liddell Hart's definition of strategy can be found in B. H. Liddell Hart,
Strategy (New York: Praeger, 1967), 321–28.

Chapter 2: Annihilation and dislocation

Excerpts from Premier Renaud's speech are available at https://www
.foreignaffairs.com/articles/france/1940-10-01/downfall-france.
Henry Kissinger's remarks about guerrilla warfare are in Henry
Kissinger, "The Vietnam Negotiations," *Foreign Affairs* 47, no. 2
(January 1969): 212.
Liddell Hart's explanation of the indirect approach is available in
B. H. Liddell Hart, *Strategy* (New York: Praeger, 1967), 321.

Chapter 3: Attrition and exhaustion

President Roosevelt's 1943 State of the Union Address can be accessed at Gerhard Peters and John T. Woolley, *The American Presidency Project* at https://www.presidency.ucsb.edu/documents/state-the-union-address-0.

Admiral Stark's quote can be found in H. P. Willmott, *Empires in the Balance: Japanese and Allied Pacific Strategies to April 1942* (Annapolis, MD: Naval Institute Press, 1982), 84.

Admiral Yamamoto's quote can be found in Ronald Spector, *Eagle against the Sun: The American War with Japan* (New York: Vintage, 1985), 64–65.

The Gallup Poll of American opinion of U.S. involvement in the Vietnam war from August 27, 1965, to November 13, 1968; see Hazel Erskine, "The Polls: Is War a Mistake?" *Public Opinion Quarterly* 34, no. 1 (Spring 1970): 134–70.

Chapter 4: Deterrence and compellence

For Henry Kissinger's comment regarding deterrence, see Henry Kissinger, *Diplomacy* (New York: Simon & Shuster, 1994), 608.

Schelling's reference to "vicious" diplomacy is found in Thomas C. Schelling, *Arms and Influence* (New Haven, CT: Yale University Press, 1966), 2.

Chapter 5: Terror and terrorism

On Mao's ideas concerning the value of terror to guerrilla warfare, see Mao Tse-tung, "Report of an Investigation into the Peasant Movement in Hunan," in *Selected Works of Mao Tse-tung*, vol. 1 (London: International Publishers, 1954), 27.

On Che's comments regarding the counterproductive nature of terror, see Jon Lee Anderson, *Che Guevara: A Revolutionary Life*, rev. ed. (New York: Grove, 1997), 448.

On Lenin's views of the utility of terror, see V. I. Lenin, "The Lessons of the Moscow Uprising" (1906), in *Lenin: Collected Works*, vol. 11 (Moscow: Progress, 1965), 176.

Chapter 6: Decapitation and targeted killing

Hugh Trenchard's comments about the moral effects of bombing can be found at Anon., "Bombing Germany: General Trenchard's Report of Operations of British Airmen against German Cities," *New York Times Current History*, April 1919, 151–56.

Chapter 7: Winning without fighting: information and cyber power

For the groundbreaking article on cognitive biases by Amos Tversky and Daniel Kahneman, see "Judgment under Uncertainty: Heuristics and Biases." *Science* 185, no. 4157 (September 27, 1974); 1124–31.

On data from Oxford's Internet Institute, see Philip N. Howard, *Lie Machines: How to Save Democracy from Troll Armies, Deceitful Robots, Junk News Operations, and Political Operatives* (New Haven, CT: Yale University Press, 2020), 45–51.

On Russia's Internet Research Agency (IRA), see Krishnadev Calamur, "What Is the Internet Research Agency? The Origin of the Russian 'Troll Farm' That Allegedly Targeted America's 2016 Presidential Election." *The Atlantic*. February 16, 2018.

On "reflexive control," see Timothy L. Thomas, "Russia's Reflexive Control Theory and the Military," *Journal of Slavic Military Studies* 17, no. 2 (August 2010): 237–56. https://www.tandfonline.com/toc/fslv20/17/2?nav=tocList.

Further reading

Allmand, Christopher. *The 'De Re Military' of Vegetius. The Reception, Transmission and Legacy of a Roman Text in the Middle Ages.* Cambridge, UK: Cambridge University Press, 2011.

Anderson, David L., and John Ernst, eds. *The War That Never Ends: New Perspectives on the Vietnam War.* Lexington: University Press of Kentucky, 2014.

Anderson, Jon Lee. *Che Guevara: A Revolutionary Life.* Rev. ed. New York: Grove, 1997.

Anon. "Bombing Germany: General Trenchard's Report of Operations of British Airmen against German Cities." *New York Times Current History*, April 1919, 151–56.

Armstrong, Hamilton Fish. "The Downfall of France." *Foreign Affairs* 19, no. 1 (October 1940): 55–144.

Beaufre, André. *An Introduction to Strategy.* Paris: Colin, 1963.

Beevor, Anthony. *The Second World War.* New York: Little, Brown, 2013.

Benkler, Yochai, Robert Faris, and Hal Roberts. *Network Propaganda: Manipulation, Disinformation, and Radicalization in American Politics.* New York: Oxford University Press, 2018.

Betts, Richard K. "Is Strategy an Illusion?" *International Security* 25, no. 2 (Fall 2000): 5–50.

Biddle, Stephen. *Military Power: Explaining Victory and Defeat in Modern Battle.* Princeton, NJ: Princeton University Press, 2004.

Bond, Brian. *Liddell Hart: A Study of His Military Thought.* New Brunswick, NJ: Rutgers University Press, 1977.

Brodie, Bernard. *The Absolute Weapon.* New York: Harcourt, Brace, 1946.

Bullock, Alan. *Hitler: A Study in Tyranny*. Rev. ed. New York: Harper, 1964.

Bungay, Stephen. *The Most Dangerous Enemy: A History of the Battle of Britain*. London: Aurum, 2001.

Byman, Daniel, and Matthew Waxman. *The Dynamics of Coercion: American Foreign Policy and the Limits of Military Might*. Cambridge, UK: Cambridge University Press, 2002.

Carr, Jeffrey. *Inside Cyber Warfare*. 2d ed. Sebastopol, CA: O'Reilly Media, 2012.

Casey, Steven. *When Soldiers Fall: How Americans Have Confronted Combat Losses from World War I to Afghanistan*. Oxford: Oxford University Press, 2013.

Chandler, David G. *The Campaigns of Napoleon*. New York: Macmillan, 1966.

Clapper, James R. "*Statement for the Record: Worldwide Threat Assessment of the U.S. Intelligence Community: Senate Select Committee on Intelligence*," January 29, 2014; 2014 WWTA SFR_SSCI_29_Jan.pdf (dni.gov). https://www.dni.gov/files/documents/Intelligence%20Reports/2014%20WWTA%20%20SFR_SSCI_29_Jan.pdf

Clarke, Richard A. *Cyber War: The Next Threat to National Security and What to Do about It*. New York: Ecco Press, 2010.

Clausewitz, Carl von. *On War*. Translated and edited by Michael Howard and Peter Paret. Princeton, NJ: Princeton University Press, 1986.

Corum, James S. *The Roots of Blitzkrieg: Hans von Seeckt and German Military Reform*. Lawrence: University Press of Kansas, 1992.

Craig, Gordon A., and Alexander L. George. *Force and Statecraft: Diplomatic Problems in Our Time*. 2d ed. Oxford: Oxford University Press, 1990.

Cronin, Audrey Kurth. *How Terrorism Ends: Understanding the Decline and Demise of Terrorist Campaigns*. Princeton, NJ: Princeton University Press, 2009.

Danchev, Alex. *Alchemist of War: The Life of Basil Liddell Hart*. London: Nicholson, 1998.

Davis, Lance E., and Stanley L. Engerman. *Naval Blockades in Peace and War: An Economic History since 1750*. Cambridge, UK: Cambridge University Press, 2006.

Detter, Ingrid. *The Law of War*. 3rd ed. Burlington, VT: Ashgate, 2013.

Duffy, Christopher. *Austerlitz 1805*. London: Seeley, 1977.

Duiker, William J. *Ho Chi Minh: A Life*. New York: Hyperion, 2000.

Dupuy, Trevor N. *Numbers, Predictions, and War: Using History to Evaluate Combat Factors and Predict the Outcome of Battles.* Indianapolis: Bobbs-Merrill, 1979.

Ellis, John. *Brute Force: Allied Strategy and Tactics in the Second World War.* New York: Viking, 1990.

Everett, Anthony. *The Rise of Rome: The Making of the World's Greatest Empire.* New York: Random House, 2014.

Finkelstein, Claire, Jens David Ohlin, and Andrew Altman, eds. *Targeted Killings: Law and Morality in an Asymmetrical World.* Oxford: Oxford University Press, 2012.

Freedman, Lawrence. *Deterrence.* Cambridge, UK: Polity, 2004.

Freedman, Lawrence. *The Evolution of Nuclear Strategy.* 3rd ed. New York: Palgrave, 2003.

Freedman, Lawrence, ed. *Strategic Coercion.* Oxford: Oxford University Press, 1998.

Freedman, Lawrence. *Strategy: A History.* Oxford: Oxford University Press, 2013.

Frieser, Karl-Heinz. *The Blitzkrieg Legend.* Annapolis, MD: Naval Institute Press, 2005.

Gaddis, John Lewis. *Strategies of Containment: A Critical Appraisal of American National Security Policy during the Cold War.* Rev. ed. Oxford: Oxford University Press, 2005.

Galula, David. *Counterinsurgency Warfare: Theory and Practice, 1964.* Reprint. Westport, CT: Praeger, 2006.

George, Alexander L. *Forceful Persuasion: Coercive Diplomacy as an Alternative to War.* Washington, DC: U.S. Institute of Peace, 1997.

Goldsworthy, Adrian. *The Fall of Carthage: The Punic Wars, 265–146 BC.* London: Cassell, 2000.

Graham, Dominic. *Tug of War: The Battle for Italy, 1943–45.* New York: St. Martin's, 1986.

Gray, Colin. *The Strategy Bridge: Theory for Practice.* Oxford: Oxford University Press, 2010.

Guevara, Che *Guerrilla Warfare.* 3rd ed. Edited by Brian Loveman and Thomas M. Davies Jr. Wilmington, DE: Scholarly Resources, 1997.

Gunaratna, Rohan, ed. *The Changing Face of Terrorism.* Singapore: Eastern Universities Press, 2004.

Hammond, Grant. *The Mind of War: John Boyd and American Security.* Washington, DC: Smithsonian Institution Press, 2001.

Hensel, Howard M., ed. *The Prism of Just War: Asian and Western Perspectives on the Legitimate Use of Military Force*. London: Routledge, 2016.

Heuser, Beatrice. *The Evolution of Strategy: Thinking War from Antiquity to the Present*. Cambridge, UK: Cambridge University Press, 2010.

Himes, Kenneth R. *Drones and the Ethics of Targeted Killings*. New York: Rowman & Littlefield, 2015.

Hippler, Thomas. *Bombing the People: Giulio Douhet and the Foundations of Air-Power Strategy, 1884–1939*. Cambridge, UK: Cambridge University Press, 2013.

Howard, Michael. "The Forgotten Dimensions of Strategy." In *The Causes of Wars and Other Essays*, 101–15. London: Unwin, 1983.

Howard, Philip N., and Samuel Woolley, eds., *Computational Propaganda: Political Parties, Politicians, and Political Manipulation on Social Media*. New York: Oxford University Press, 2018.

Huth, Paul K. *Extended Deterrence and the Prevention of War*. New Haven, CT: Yale University Press, 1991.

Jomini, Baron de. *The Art of War*. Translated by G. H. Mendell and W. P. Craighill. 1862. Westport, CT: Greenwood, 1971.

Jones, Archer. *Elements of Military Strategy: An Historical Approach*. Westport, CT: Greenwood, 1996.

Kahn, Herman. *On Escalation*. New York: Praeger, 1965.

Kahn, Herman. *On Thermonuclear War*. Princeton, NJ: Princeton University Press, 1960.

Kennedy, Paul, ed. *Grand Strategies in War and Peace*. New Haven, CT: Yale University Press, 1991.

Kissinger, Henry. *Diplomacy*. New York: Simon & Shuster, 1994.

Kissinger, Henry. "The Viet Nam Negotiations." *Foreign Affairs* 47, no. 2 (January 1969): 211–34.

Knuckey, Sarah. *Drones and Targeted Killings: Ethics, Law, and Politics*. New York: IDEA Publications, 2014.

Kraft, Michael, and Edward Marks. *US Government Counterterrorism: A Guide to Who Does What*. Boca Raton, FL: CRC Press, 2012.

Lebow, Richard Ned, and Janice Gross Stein. *We All Lost the Cold War*. Princeton, NJ: Princeton University Press, 1994.

Libicki, Martin. *Crisis and Escalation in Cyberspace*. Santa Monica, CA: RAND, 2012.

Liddell Hart, B. H. *Strategy*. New York: Praeger, 1967.

Liddell Hart, B. H. *The Strategy of the Indirect Approach: Decisive Wars of History*. London: Faber and Faber, 1941.

Luttwak, Edward. *Strategy*. Cambridge, MA: Harvard University Press, 1987.

Lykke, Arthur F. Jr. "Toward an Understanding of Military Strategy." In *Military Strategy: Theory and Application*. Carlisle, PA: U.S. Army War College, 1989, pp. 179–85.

Machiavelli, Niccolò. *The Art of War*. Translated by Ellis Farnesworth. New York: Da Capo, 1990.

Machiavelli, Niccolò. *The Prince*. Translated and edited by David Wooton. Indianapolis: Hackett, 1995.

Mao Tse-tung. *Selected Military Writings*. Peking: Foreign Language Press, 1963.

Mao Tse-tung. *Selected Works of Mao Tse-tung*. London: International Publishers, 1954.

Mearsheimer, John J. *Liddell Hart and the Weight of History*. Ithaca, NY: Cornell University Press, 1988.

Meilinger, Phillip S., ed. *The Paths of Heaven: The Evolution of Airpower Theory*. Maxwell, AL: Air University Press, 2001.

Melzer, Nils. *Targeted Killing in International Law*. Oxford: Oxford University Press, 2008.

Mitchell, William. *Winged Defense: The Development and Possibilities of Modern Airpower—Economic and Military*. New York: Putnam's, 1925.

Murray, Williamson, and Allan Millett. *A War to Be Won: Fighting the Second World War*. Cambridge, MA: Harvard University Press, 2000.

Murray, Williamson, and Richard Hart Sinnreich, eds. *Successful Strategies: Triumphing in War and Peace from Antiquity to the Present*. Cambridge, UK: Cambridge University Press, 2014.

O'Brien, Phillips Payson. *How the War Was Won: Air-Sea Power and Allied Victory in World War II*. Cambridge, UK: Cambridge University Press, 2014.

Olsen, John Andreas. *John Warden and the Renaissance of American Air Power*. Washington, DC: Potomac, 2007.

Osgood, Robert E. *Limited War: The Challenge to American Strategy*. Chicago: University of Chicago Press, 1957.

Osgood, Robert E. *Limited War Revisited*. Boulder, CO: Westview, 1979.

Osinga, Frans. *Science, Strategy, and War: The Strategic Theory of John Boyd*. London: Routledge, 2006.

Overy, Richard. *The Battle of Britain: The Myth and Reality*. New York: W. W. Norton, 2002.

Panetta, Leon E. "Defending the Nation from Cyber Attack," October 11, 2012, Business Executives for National Security, New York.

Pape, Robert A. *Bombing to Win: Airpower and Coercion in War.* Ithaca, NY: Cornell University Press, 1996.

Payne, Keith B. *Deterrence in the Second Nuclear Age.* Lexington: University Press of Kentucky, 1996.

Payne, Keith B. *The Great American Gamble: Deterrence Theory and Practice from the Cold War to the Twenty-First Century.* Fairfax, VA: National Institute, 2008.

Pomerantsev, Peter. *This Is Not Propaganda: Adventures in the War against Reality.* New York: Faber, 2019.

Porch, Douglas. *Counterinsurgency: Exposing the Myths of the New Way of War.* Cambridge, UK: Cambridge University Press, 2013.

Powers, Shawn M., and Michael Jablonski. *The Real Cyber War: The Political Economy of Internet Freedom.* Urbana: University of Illinois Press, 2015.

Reilly, Henry J. "Blitzkrieg" *Foreign Affairs* 18, no. 2 (January 1940): 254–65.

Rickards, James. *Currency Wars: The Making of the Next Global Crisis.* New York: Penguin, 2011.

Rid, Thomas. *Active Measures: The Secret History of Disinformation and Political Warfare.* New York: Macmillan, 2020.

Roosevelt, Franklin D. "State of the Union Address," January 7, 1943. In *The American Presidency Project.* By Gerhard Peters and John T. Woolley. University of California, Santa Barbara. https://www.presidency.ucsb.edu/documents/state-the-union-address-0.

Schelling, Thomas C. *Arms and Influence.* New Haven, CT: Yale University Press, 1966.

Schelling, Thomas C. *The Strategy of Conflict.* Cambridge, MA: Harvard University Press, 1960.

Shakarian, Paulo, Jana Shakarian, and Andrew Ruef. *Introduction to Cyber-warfare: A Multidisciplinary Approach.* Waltham, MA: Syngress, 2013.

Short, Philip. *Mao: A Life.* New York: Henry Holt, 1999.

Singer, Peter, and Emerson T. Brooking. *Like War: The Weaponization of Social Media.* New York: Houghton Mifflin, 2018.

Slessor, John. *Airpower and Armies.* London: University of Oxford Press, 1936.

Stoler, Mark. *Allies and Adversaries: The Joint Chiefs of Staff, the Grand Alliance, and US Strategy in World War II.* Chapel Hill and London: University of North Carolina Press, 2000.

Strachan, Hew. *The Direction of War: Contemporary Strategy in Historical Perspective*. Cambridge, UK: Cambridge University Press, 2013.

Summers, Harry G. Jr. *On Strategy: A Critical Analysis of the Vietnam War*. Novato, CA: Presidio, 2018.

Summers, Harry Jr. *On Strategy II: A Critical Analysis of the Gulf War*. New York: Dell, 1992.

Sun-tzu, *The Art of War*. Trans. Samuel B. Griffith. New York: Oxford University Press, 1994.

United Nations. *The UN General Assembly, Report of the Special Rapporteur on Extrajudicial, Summary or Arbitrary Executions, May 28, 2010*. New York: United Nations.

United States Strategic Bombing Survey, Summary Report, European War. Washington, DC: U.S. Government Printing Office, 1945.

United States Strategic Bombing Survey. Summary Report, Pacific War. Washington, DC: U.S. Government Printing Office, 1946.

Valeriano, Brandon, and Ryan C. Maness. *Cyber War versus Cyber Realities: Cyber Conflict in the International System*. New York: Oxford University Press, 2015.

Walzer, Michael. *Just and Unjust Wars: A Moral Argument with Historical Illustrations*. 5th ed. New York: Basic Books, 2015.

Warden, John A. III. *Air Campaign: Planning for Combat*. Washington, DC: National Defense University, 1989.

Wells, H. G. *The War in the Air*. New York: Macmillan, 1908.

Willmott, H. P. *Empires in the Balance: Japanese and Allied Pacific Strategies to April 1942*. Annapolis, MD: Naval Institute Press, 1982.

Wilner, Alex S. *Deterring Rational Fanatics*. Philadelphia: University of Pennsylvania Press, 2015.

Wohlstetter, Albert. *The Delicate Balance of Terror*. Santa Monica, CA: Rand Corp., 1958.

Young, Oran. *The Politics of Force: Bargaining during International Crises*. Princeton, NJ: Princeton University Press, 1968.

Zarate, Juan C. *Treasury's War: The Unleashing of a New Era of Financial Warfare*. New York: Public Affairs, 2013.

Index

ALEXANDER THE GREAT
A Very Short Introduction
Hugh Bowden

Alexander the Great became king of Macedon in 336 BC, when he was only 20 years old, and died at the age of 32, twelve years later. During his reign he conquered the Achaemenid Persian Empire, the largest empire that had ever existed, leading his army from Greece to Pakistan, and from the Libyan desert to the steppes of Central Asia. His meteoric career, as leader of an alliance of Greek cities, Pharaoh of Egypt, and King of Persia, had a profound effect on the world he moved through. Even in his lifetime his achievements became legendary and in the centuries that following his story was told and retold throughout Europe and the East. Greek became the language of power in the Eastern Mediterranean and much of the Near East, as powerful Macedonian dynasts carved up Alexander's empire into kingdoms of their own, underlaying the flourishing Hellenistic civilization that emerged after his death.

But what do we really know about Alexander? In this *Very Short Introduction*, Hugh Bowden goes behind the usual historical accounts of Alexander's life and career. Instead, he focuses on the evidence from Alexander's own time—letters from officials in Afghanistan, Babylonian diaries, records from Egyptian temples—to try and understand how Alexander appeared to those who encountered him. In doing so he also demonstrates the profound influence the legends of his life have had on our historical understanding and the controversy they continue to generate worldwide.

www.oup.com/vsi

DIPLOMACY
A Very Short Introduction
Joseph M. Siracusa

Like making war, diplomacy has been around a very long time, at least since the Bronze Age. It was primitive by today's standards, there were few rules, but it was a recognizable form of diplomacy. Since then, diplomacy has evolved greatly, coming to mean different things, to different persons, at different times, ranging from the elegant to the inelegant. Whatever one's definition, few could doubt that the course and consequences of the major events of modern international diplomacy have shaped and changed the global world in which we live. Joseph M. Siracusa introduces the subject of diplomacy from a historical perspective, providing examples from significant historical phases and episodes to illustrate the art of diplomacy in action.

'Professor Siracusa provides a lively introduction to diplomacy through the perspective of history.'

Gerry Woodard, Senior Fellow in Political Science at the University of Melbourne and former Australasian Ambassador in Asia

GEOPOLITICS
A Very Short Introduction
Klaus Dodds

In certain places such as Iraq or Lebanon, moving a few
feet either side of a territorial boundary can be a matter of life
or death, dramatically highlighting the connections between
place and politics. For a country's location and size as well as
its sovereignty and resources all affect how the people that live
there understand and interact with the wider world. Using
wide-ranging examples, from historical maps to James Bond
films and the rhetoric of political leaders like Churchill and
George W. Bush, this Very Short Introduction shows why,
for a full understanding of contemporary global politics, it is
not just smart - it is essential - to be geopolitical.

'Engrossing study of a complex topic.'

Mick Herron, Geographical.

HUMAN RIGHTS
A Very Short Introduction
Andrew Clapham

An appeal to human rights in the face of injustice can be a heartfelt and morally justified demand for some, while for others it remains merely an empty slogan. Taking an international perspective and focusing on highly topical issues such as torture, arbitrary detention, privacy, health and discrimination, this *Very Short Introduction* will help readers to understand for themselves the controversies and complexities behind this vitally relevant issue. Looking at the philosophical justification for rights, the historical origins of human rights and how they are formed in law, Andrew Clapham explains what our human rights actually are, what they might be, and where the human rights movement is heading.

www.oup.com/vsi

NUCLEAR WEAPONS
A Very Short Introduction
Joseph M. Siracusa

In this *Very Short Introduction*, the history and politics of the bomb are explained: from the technology of nuclear weapons, to the revolutionary implications of the H-bomb, and the politics of nuclear deterrence. The issues are set against a backdrop of the changing international landscape, from the early days of development, through the Cold War, to the present-day controversy of George W. Bush's National Missile Defence, and the threat and role of nuclear weapons in the so-called Age of Terror. Joseph M. Siracusa provides a comprehensive, accessible, and at times chilling overview of the most deadly weapon ever invented.

www.oup.com/vsi

TERRORISM
A Very Short Introduction
Charles Townshend

What is terrorism? Is terrorism crime or war? What can we do to
stop it?

In this *Very Short Introduction*, Charles Townshend unravels the
questions at the heart of the problem of terrorism. He details the
impact and consequences of terrorism through exploration into
recent terror attacks including those in Brussels, Paris, Nice, and
Rouen. Looking at recent terrorism, Townshend discusses the
emergence of ISIS, the significant rise in individual suicide, and the
issue of 'cyberterror'. As well as answering central questions in
regard to terrorism, he also details counterterrorist measures used
by authorities, ranging from control orders to drone strikes.

THE FIRST WORLD WAR
A Very Short Introduction
Michael Howard

By the time the First World War ended in 1918, eight million people had died in what had been perhaps the most apocalyptic episode the world had known. This *Very Short Introduction* provides a concise and insightful history of the 'Great War', focusing on why it happened, how it was fought, and why it had the consequences it did. It examines the state of Europe in 1914 and the outbreak of war; the onset of attrition and crisis; the role of the US; the collapse of Russia; and the weakening and eventual surrender of the Central Powers. Looking at the historical controversies surrounding the causes and conduct of war, Michael Howard also describes how peace was ultimately made, and the potent legacy of resentment left to Germany.

'succinct, comprehensive and beautifully written. Indeed reading it is an experience comparable to scanning the clues of a well-composed crossword puzzle. Every allusion is eventually supplied with an answer, and the finished product defies the puzzler's disbelief that the intricacies can be brought to a convincing conclusion.... Michael Howard is the master of the short book'

TLS